MARCO ⊕ POLO

Travel with **Insider Tips**

BALI

LOMBOK, GILI ISLANDS

Vietnam
Ho Chi Minh
City

PHILIPPINES

Palawan

Mindanao

Kuala
Lumpur

Brunei

MALAYSIA

Singapore

Equator   Kalimantan
(Borneo)

Moluccas

Sumatra

Sulawesi

INDONESIA

(Celebes)

Jakarta

Java

Lombok

Bali

Flores

Timor

D0348102

www.marco-polo.com

The best Insider Tips → p. 4

INSIDER TIP

Best of ... → p. 6

Bali → p. 32

Lombok → p. 74

SYMBOLS

INSIDER TIP	Insider Tip
★	Highlight
●●●●	Best of ...
☼	Scenic view
☺	Responsible travel: fair trade principles and the environment respected

PRICE CATEGORIES HOTELS

Expensive over 1,900,000 Rp

Moderate 800,000 Rp–1,900,000 Rp

Budget under 800,000 Rp

The prices are for a double room with breakfast

PRICE CATEGORIES RESTAURANTS

Expensive over 175,000 Rp

Moderate 80,000 Rp–175,000 Rp

Budget under 80,000 Rp

The prices are for a dinner with a starter and main course

On the cover: Breathtaking views from the summit p. 72 | Gili Trawangan is a party paradise p. 95

CONTENTS

Gili Islands → p. 90

Trips & Tours → p. 98

Sports & Activities → p. 104

Road atlas → p. 126

DID YOU KNOW?

Timeline → p. 12
Local specialities → p. 26
Books & Films → p. 57
Volcanoes → p. 69
Budgeting → p. 115
Currency converter → p. 117
Weather in Denpasar
→ p. 119
Indonesian: Pronunciation
→ p. 120

MAPS IN THE GUIDEBOOK

(128 A1) Page numbers
and coordinates refer to
the road atlas
(O) Site/address located
off the map
Coordinates are also given
for places that are not
marked on the road atlas
(U A1) refers to the map of
Kuta inside the back cover

**INSIDE BACK COVER:
PULL-OUT MAP →**

PULL-OUT MAP ⬦

(⬦ A1) Refers to the
removable pull-out map
(⬦ a–b 2–3) Refers to
additional inset maps on the
pull-out map

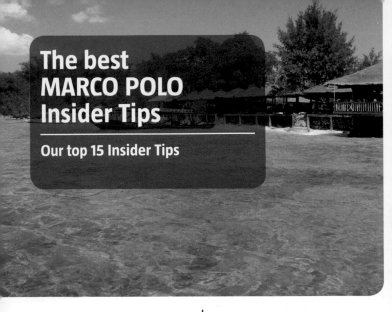

The best MARCO POLO Insider Tips

Our top 15 Insider Tips

INSIDER TIP Literature in the heart of Bali

Small but excellent: the Ubud Writers & Readers Festival is one of the world's most intimate literature festivals with a very special atmosphere → **p. 111**

INSIDER TIP Cocktails on the rocks

360-degree panorama, 14m (46ft) above the sea: Bali experts feel that the design and music in the Rock Bar of the Ayana Resort make it one of the best locations on the island → **p. 38**

INSIDER TIP Village idyll in the highlands of Bali

Enjoy the fresh mountain air, lush nature and a great deal of tranquillity in the Puri Lumbung Cottages in the small village of Munduk on Lake Tamblingan → **p. 51**

INSIDER TIP Private villa in the fishing village

The Kampung resort has holiday cottages in traditional Javanese style right on the beach at Amed: relax and watch the colourful outriggers → **p. 36**

INSIDER TIP Jungle and mangroves

The national park jungle and Bali's best diving region are right on the doorstep of The Menjangan lifestyle resort → **p. 56**

INSIDER TIP Wallow in nostalgia

The Biku Tea Lounge in Seminyak serves traditional colonial style afternoon tea – classically English or with tasty delicacies from all over Asia → **p. 62**

INSIDER TIP Far Eastern wellness temple

Indulge at Seminyak's Private Spa Wellness Center: Asian massages, a dip in the bio-thermal pool or a session in the herbal steam bath decorated in oriental style → **p. 63**

INSIDER TIP Meditation and lifestyle

Not only for yogis: yoga and meditation are not the only highlights at the Bali Spirit Festival in Ubud; you will find dance and music from around the world on every corner → **p. 66**

→ **p. 66**

INSIDER**TIP** **Fairytale beach between the cliffs**

Overnight in Selong Belanak: the cliffs are bathed in bewitching light at dawn and dusk → **p. 78**

INSIDER**TIP** **Sunset beneath the palms**

Genuine island feeling on the beach of the unspoilt Exile Resort: you will have Trawangan's best view of the sunset from here → **p. 97**

INSIDER**TIP** **Chill out at a coral reef**

Go snorkelling straight from the beach and then enjoy delicious cocktails and tapas in the Adeng-Adeng Beach Bar on Gili Meno (photo left) → **p. 94**

INSIDER**TIP** **Underwater adventure**

Explore the spectacular underwater world off the coast of Lombok's little-visited Sekotong Peninsula with diving instructors from Divezone → **p. 83**

INSIDER**TIP** **Between the volcano and the sea**

Stressed tourists can relax and recharge their batteries surrounded by pristine nature: the Rinjani Mountain Garden offers idyllic highland surroundings, a natural swimming pool and panoramic views that stretch from the Rinjani Volcano to the Pacific Ocean → **p. 84**

INSIDER**TIP** **Through the rice fields on a bicycle**

Authentic village life, verdant rice fields, jungle and plantations full of tropical fruit will accompany you on the novel tours organised by Mountain Bike Lombok and they are also not too strenuous for average cyclists → **p. 106**

INSIDER**TIP** **Dance and play music like the Balinese**

Professional gamelan and dance courses for children and adults are held in the studio of the Mekar Bhuana Conservatory in Denpasar (photo below) → **p. 109**

BEST OF ...

FOR FREE

● **Free cocktails in the nightclub**
Some nightclubs in the south of Bali serve free cocktails at certain times: such as the *Sky Garden Lounge* that offers gratis cocktails and snacks for one hour starting at 11pm → p. 47

● **Free art in galleries**
Not interested in museums? You can admire Balinese painting and sculptures on your foray into *Ubud's art galleries* – there is no charge for admission and you will often even be served coffee → p. 67

● **Turtles on the beach**
Turtle stations, such as the one on Gili Trawangan, are open for all and the people working there will be happy to tell you about the rescue of these marine creatures threatened by extinction → p. 95

● **No visit to a temple without a sarong**
Wear your own wrap-around sarong, which you can buy inexpensively at the market or in a souvenir shop, when you *visit a temple.* That way you save the money spent hiring a sash and sarong → p. 71

● **Sasak handicraft villages**
In Banyumulek and Sukarara, you will be able to go into the workshops *of the potters and weavers* and watch the craftspeople at work. It is then left up to you to decide if you want to buy something in the shop → p. 89

● **Dance in the museum**
Children from various villages practice their dance every Saturday at 4pm in the inner courtyards of the *Bali Museum* in Denpasar – and you will be able to watch them for free → p. 43

● **Performances at the temple festival**
Gamelan, dance and shadow theatre are part of every temple anniversary. Instead of buying tickets for a tourist show, just ask where the next *Odalan festival* is being held (photo) – tourists are welcome if they behave properly → p. 110

●●●● Dots in guidebook refer to 'Best of ...' tips

● *World Cultural Heritage in the rice field*
The Subak system – the irrigation concept of Bali's rice terraces – is characterised by democratic and egalitarian principles, as well as harmony between the spiritual world and man and nature. This cultural heritage is clearly explained in the *Subak Museum* in Tabanan → **p. 101**

● *Giant lizards and dwarf deer*
The dividing line between the Asian and Austronesian primeval continents runs between Bali and Lombok and the flora and fauna of both continents mix here. You will get a particularly good impression of the unique animal and plant world in the *Rinjani National Park* (photo) – also possible on easy day tours; you don't have to climb the peak straight away! → **p. 85**

● *Colourful processions*
Women dressed in brightly-coloured clothes balance fruit pyramids on their heads; the men beat heavy gongs: on Bali, you never know when you are going to come across a procession. The most impressive are the parades celebrating the *Galungan Festival* → **p. 110**

● *Between volcanoes and coral reefs*
Something you can only experience on the Gilis – and best of all, on the small hill on *Gili Trawangan:* the Gunung Rijani rises up in the east at dawn and the Gunung Agung shows just how big it is in the west at sunset. In the hours in between, you can explore the fantastic underwater mountains of the coral islands → **p. 95**

● *Spicy poultry*
The way the locals like it: the simple *Lesehan Taliwang Irama Restaurant* in Mataram, which is very popular with the Indonesians, serves a no frills, tasty chilli chicken → **p. 80**

● *The battle of the packets of rice*
During *Perang Topat* – which always takes place at the beginning of the rainy season in Pura Lingsar – Hindus and Muslim Sasak pelt each other with rice wrapped in palm leaves. The so-called 'Rice Cake War' is a celebration for all those involved, no matter which religion they belong to → **pp. 82, 111**

ONLY IN

BEST OF ...

AND IF IT RAINS?
Activities to brighten your day

● **Art in Nusa Dua**
Immerse yourselves in the magnificent collection of Southeast Asian and Pacific art in the *Museum Pasifika* in Nusa Dua, presented in modern Balinese architecture → p. 37

● **Balinese wine tasting**
There are also vineyards on the island of the gods – you can try the locally produced tipple at the daily tastings in the *Cellardoor* in Kuta → p. 45

● **Feel like a blockbuster?**
Instead of squinting at the poorly copied pirate DVDs in your hotel room on a rainy day, you can sink back into the chairs of the *Beachwalk XXI Premiere* and watch the latest Hollywood and Bollywood blockbusters – as well as Indonesian films – on the big screen → p. 47

● **Shopping spree at the mall**
The modern *Discovery Shopping Mall* in Kuta not only has cafés and outlets of global fashion and cosmetics companies but also Balinese designer boutiques and high-quality arts and crafts from the region → p. 45

● **Exotic arts**
You can learn exactly how the Balinese dance and play gamelan instruments, carve, create batiks and make offerings (photo) in the cultural courses offered by the *ARMA Museum* in Ubud → pp. 66, 70

● **Provincial customs**
Learn how the Sasak marry or how they make daggers in the *Museum Nusa Tenggara Barat*: here you can find out all there is to know about the history, traditions and customs of the islands of Lombok and Sumbawa that form the West Nusa Tenggara Province → p. 80

RELAX AND CHILL OUT
Take it easy and spoil yourself

● *Elegant sundowners*
When the sinking sun colours the sea orange-red, the time has arrived to order a cocktail in the chic beach restaurant of the *Mahamaya Boutique Resort* on Gili Meno → **p. 94**

● *Oriental wellness palace*
Treat yourself to a day at the luxurious *Prana Spa* in Seminyak: Ayurveda treatments, Balinese herbal scrubs, reflexology and Turkish steam baths are all on offer → **p. 63**

● *Relax on a picturesque coast*
The tranquil *Seraya Shores Resort* is far removed from the tourist route on the picturesque steep coast of eastern Bali: lose track time in the airy villas, float in the pool above the ocean and delight in the resort's delicious meals → **p. 37**

● *Yoga holiday without peer pressure*
The small *White Lotus* yoga and meditation centre offers laid-back holidays in a private atmosphere; within walking distance from the centre of Ubud and the murmuring river and view of the rice fields are included in the price → **p. 70**

● *Café on the cliffs*
High above Kuta is the *Ashtari* café and its comfortable cushions, reading corner, vegetarian delicacies and wonderful views over the south coast of Lombok will make you want to spend many hours here → **p. 77**

● *Peace in the rice field*
Let the world pass by in a bamboo pavilion in the middle of a rice field, swim at a waterfall or simply enjoy the view – you can do all of this in *Tetebatu* south of the Rinjani → **p. 82**

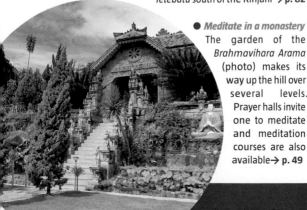

● *Meditate in a monastery*
The garden of the *Brahmavihara Arama* (photo) makes its way up the hill over several levels. Prayer halls invite one to meditate and meditation courses are also available → **p. 49**

INTRODUCTION

DISCOVER BALI, LOMBOK AND THE GILI ISLANDS!

Bali, Lombok or the Gilis – the names alone conjure up images of beaches lined with palm trees, coral reefs, of rice terraces and mighty volcanoes. Surfers, divers and mountaineers will find their paradise here, while the tourist centres offer all the amenities, from five-star restaurants to oriental spas.

Bali's unique culture draws travellers from all around the world: there are very few places where so much natural beauty meets with such a charming lifestyle as here on the 'Island of the Gods'. Surfers find perfect waves rolling in beneath the picturesque cliffs and white sandy beaches in the south of the island. A massive mountain range with deep canyons and thundering waterfalls – crowned by the 3148m (10,328ft) high active volcano, the Gunung Agung, the sacred mountain of the Balinese – towers up in the centre of the island. The verdant green of the rice terraces covers the steep mountain slopes. The more rugged northern section of the island is lined with beaches

Photo: Grass harvest on the rice terraces

Solemn ceremony: people in a procession to a temple

of black lava along the peaceful coast; the offshore reefs are home to a colourful underwater world.

Bali has preserved its unique charm

The lush nature, as well as the unique ancient Hindu culture of the island in the Indian Ocean, has fascinated travellers from the West since the 1920s, and yet, in spite of mass tourism, Bali has retained its own unique charm. As soon as they arrive at the airport, visitors are welcomed with the gentle tones of gamelan music and the aroma of clove cigarette smoke. On the ride to the hotel, they can see women by the wayside, dressed in their sarongs, artfully arranging artistically woven small baskets of rice and flowers to protect their homes from demons while motorcycles rattle past.

The first thing the hotel staff do in the morning is to make an offering to the house gods: with their sashes wrapped around them and flowers in their hair, they carry trays of fruit and incense to stone altars, junctions and doorways. These offerings and

From the 1st century
Indian and Chinese merchants bring Hindu and Buddhist influences

1478
The Hindu Majapahit Empire on Java collapses under Islam; the successor to the throne flees to Bali and establishes a new dynasty

16th century
Merchants from Sulawesi bring Islam to Lombok

1597
Beginning of Dutch colonisation

17th century
Balinese conquer Lombok

prayers are intended to appease the gods and demons – and thus protect the guests from harm.

These rituals are not staged for tourists; they are part of everyday life on Bali. The processions on feast days are even more impressive: elegantly dressed Balinese

> **Rituals are part of Balinese daily life**

women balance elaborate towers of fruit and flowers on their heads accompanied by the booming sounds of gongs. When they take part in the ceremonies in the village temples, the surf instructor with his dreadlocks and the banker from Bali's capital Denpasar both put on the traditional headdress. In some villages, the indigenous Balinese – the Bali Aga – still live according to their old animistic lifestyle.

Bali, with its traditional rites and customs, is not only the last Hindu province in Indonesia – the country with the largest Islamic population in the world – but also the most cosmopolitan island in the vast archipelago. Most Balinese speak at least a little English and tourists are welcome at most ceremonies. There are good reasons for this: tourism, from which almost 80 per cent of the barely 4 million Balinese live, is not least responsible for the fact that the island's Hindu culture has managed to survive so well. Dances, music and handicrafts not only fulfil religious purposes but are also a source of income. The government has systematically supported this since the 1960s. That is when hippies took over Bali's beaches with their surfboards and campfires.

The first foreigners to land here were the Dutch. In the middle of the 19th century this turned into a takeover but the Balinese put up fierce resistance: some of the unequal

1846/94
Start of the Dutch occupation of Bali and Lombok

1906/08
Puputan (ritual mass suicide) of Balinese royal courts to avoid colonisation

1942–45
Japan occupies Indonesia

17 August 1945
Indonesia's declaration of independence

1945–48
War of Independence against the Dutch

1955
First free elections; Sukarno named president

battles ended in the ritual suicide of entire royal courts who did not want to subjugate themselves. The Dutch colonial masters were expelled by the Japanese in the Second World War. In 1949 Bali joined the Republic of Indonesia with Lombok following one year later.

The first Indonesian President Sukarno was faced with the difficult task of forming a single democratic state out of the more than 17,000 islands of the Indonesian archipelago with their different languages, religions and cultures. The attempt ended when the military, under the leadership of General Suharto, took over power in 1965 after it had prevented an alleged coup by the Communist Party. Suharto was forced to resign after protests in 1998. Since then, several heads of government have attempted to promote the democratisation process in the largest country in Southeast Asia, which is still plagued by corruption.

Due to their special cultural position, the Balinese often feel unaffected by national politics. However, the entire nation was shaken when Islamist suicide attackers exploded bombs in front of nightclubs and tourist restaurants in 2002 and 2005. After the initial shock, the Balinese did all they could to regain the confidence of their guests. Security measures were stepped up and the travel organisations responded with new offers: ecotourism for environmentally-conscious travellers, as well as luxurious holidays in secluded villa complexes. In this way, a new scene, with Bali as a centre for spas, meditation and yoga, has developed over recent years. Ubud and Seminyak in particular have experienced a real boom in the market for organic produce, wellness offers and yoga retreats.

These developments are only slowly starting to make an impact on the Muslim dominated neighbouring island of Lombok. International tourism did not discover the island to the east of Bali until the 1980s and there is only a good tourist infrastructure on its western coast. However, following the opening of the new international airport in 2011, an increasing number of investors have announced construction projects on the south coast and there has been a rapid increase in the number of hotels, restaurants and tour operators. The three Gili Islands off the northwest coast are still the main attraction: they are a stamping ground for seaside holidaymakers

1965
The military prevents an alleged coup; massacre of around 1 million communists

1966
General Suharto takes over the government; promotion of Bali as an international destination

1998
Following serious unrest, Suharto resigns; economic crisis

2002 and 2005
228 people killed in bomb attacks in Kuta and Jimbaran

2011
Opening of international airport on Lombok

In Indonesia, the fields are still often tilled using an ox plough

and divers from all around the world. No matter whether it is a family holiday on Gili Air, splendid isolation on Gili Meno or a party trip on Gili Trawangan – everything is possible on the once uninhabited coral islands. Numerous speedboats take tourists directly from Bali to the small car-free islands that are completely surrounded by white sand beaches and also offer a fascinating underwater world. The smaller Gili Islands off the north coast of the Sekotong Peninsula in the southwest of Lombok are still largely undeveloped but no less appealing.

The majority of the population on Lombok itself still lives off agriculture and fishing, which is precisely what makes the island so charming: it is more pristine, more natural and more exciting than its sister island, Bali. This is the right place for those with a sense of adventure.

Secluded beaches and coral reefs teeming with life

There are very few cultural sites – most date from the period of the Balinese occupation in the 18th and 19th centuries – but the secluded beaches and fabulous coral reefs more than make up for this. The breathtaking Rinjani mountain massif, which covers more than half of the island, towers up in the north. The difficult climb to the summit of the second highest volcano in Indonesia (3726m/12,224ft) takes several days but those who persevere will be rewarded with an incomparable panoramic view.

The roads are bumpy and the hotels few and far between in the dry south and east of the island. This is where Lombok's indigenous people, the Sasak, go about their frugal, traditional life. The opening of the international airport only a few miles from Kuta has led to the hope that there will be tourism development in the region. However, until that happens, backpackers, surfers and divers will continue to relish the solitude of the picturesque bays and white sandy beaches – and hope that things do not change too quickly.

WHAT'S HOT

1 On the trail

Trekking The tours organised by *JED (Jl. Kayu Jati 9 y, Seminyak, www.jed.or.id)* provide tourists with genuine insights into Bali's nature and culture. The NGO hires locals who show visitors 'their' island. In this way, traditions and long established structures are protected. Those who join Pica the trekking guide (from a Swiss NGO, *www.zukunft-fuer-kinder.ch/en/)* for an island tour will not only get an insider's view but will also support disadvantaged Balinese. Many of the tour guides were once beggars.

Fashionable 2

Trendy More and more designers from the archipelago are making a splash internationally. One of them is Lelya Wati *(www.lelya.com)*, whose luxurious handbags can also be found on the shopping streets of New York. Oka Diputra's draped and knotted designs are turning heads on the global stage *(okadiputra.net, photo)*. His dresses can be purchased in the *Istana Kuta Galeria (Jl. Patih Jelantik)*. The whacky creations of *Shaman Electro (Jl. Raya Seminyak, www.shaman-electro.com)* are perfect party wear.

3 On your feet

Active Hawaii's stand up paddling has conquered the world. It is no wonder as you will be fit in a jiffy, not get very wet and have a fine view most of the time. Above all, the trendy sport can be mastered in next to no time. You can learn how to handle a board in just a couple of hours with *Bali Stand Up Paddle (Jl. Cemara 72, Sanur, www.bali-standuppaddle.org, photo)*. Beginners start in calm waters and the experts head for the waves. *Kima Surf (Jl. Camplung Tanduk 8, Seminyak, www.kimasurf.com)* hires boards and paddles and also offers courses.

Eye-catching

Architecture Many buildings blend so well into the gentle landscape of Bali that they become almost invisible. But there are also some real eye-catchers such as the luxurious *Anantara Seminyak Resort & Spa (Jl. Pemutih, Labuan Sait, Uluwatu, photo)*. The hotel's *Wild Orchid* restaurant not only serves fabulous cuisine but also has a spectacular terrace. Overnight guests will be delighted with the floor-to-ceiling windows, the up-holstered lounging areas and the sunken terrazzo bath tubs – on the balcony. *The Bale (Jl. Raya Nusa Dua Selatan, Nusa Dua, Bali)* is made up of 29 pavilions that all stand out with their purist design. The same can be said of the complex's own restaurant: *Faces*, with Asian aromas wafting out of its open kitchen. Everybody in Singapore knows about it: with the *Alila Villas Uluwatu Resort (www.alilavillasuluwatu.com)*, Woha (www.wohadesigns.com) has also created a holistic architectural project on Bali.

Great shopping

Shopping Bali has much more than folklore to offer. Design with an Italian touch can be bought at chic *Namu (Jl. Petitenget 234 x, Petitenget)*, SKS Bali (Jl. Kayu Aya 40, Seminyak) is the place to go for cool furniture as well as clothes and the *Horn Emporium (Jl. Petitenget 100 x, Petitenget, photo)* has quite simply everything your heart desires. The things that men love – motorbikes, surfboards, art – are available from *Deus Temple (Jl. Batu Mejan 8, Canggu, www.deustemple.com)* while women will probably prefer the Australian Samantha Robinson's shop with exquisite accessories for the home *(Jl. Kayu Jati 2 A, Seminyak, samantharobinson.com.au)*.

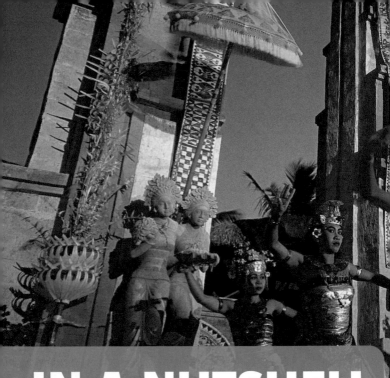

IN A NUTSHELL

CASTE SYSTEM

The caste system is still important to the Balinese. This is most apparent in the names: on the highest standing are Brahmans (priests) called *Ida Bagus* and *Ida Ayu*; *Tjokorda* or *Anak Agung* the Ksatria (warriors and nobility). Members of the Wesya caste (merchants) call themselves *Gusti*. 90 per cent of the Balinese belong to the *Sudra* (farmer) caste. They 'number' their children: the first born is named Wayan or Putu, the second child Made or Kadek, the third Nyoman or Komang and the fourth Ketut. They start numbering from the beginning once again after the fifth child. The gender distinction is that men have *I* before their name and women *Ni*.

COCKFIGHTS

Since 1982, cockfights have only been allowed for 'ritual purposes'. However, this has not prevented the Balinese from holding illegal competitions. The cocks are kept separated from each other in bell-shaped baskets, and their owners take great care of them and their training. Before the fight, sharp blades are tied to the birds' feet. The bloody spectacle is usually over in just a few seconds. In pre-Hindu times, this ritual was intended to pacify evil demons.

Photo: Balinese dance

Life on Bali, Lombok and the Gilis is determined by religions, traditions and the influence of nature

CREMATION

The Balinese believe that the soul only becomes free after the physical body has been destroyed. Elaborate cremation towers in the form of animals (such as bulls or dragons) are built for the lavish funeral rites. A ritual of this kind is a very expensive affair and many of the dead persons are buried for years – and supposedly haunt the cemetery – until the family has saved enough money to be able to afford the expensive ceremony. Poorer families often pool their resources for a mass cremation. The magnificent processions and spectacular cremations are considered major tourist attractions.

DANCE

On Bali, dances are performed on almost all occasions – at temple festivals, family ceremonies or simply for entertainment. Most of the dances are about characters from the Hindu epics *Ramayana* and *Mahabharata*. The magnificently attired dancers always remain in contact with the ground; each spread of the finger and roll of the eye has a special meaning. Short versions of the most famous dances are performed for tourists: the *barong* describes the battle between a mythical creature and the evil witch Rangda. The graceful *legong* is danced by girls before their first menstruation. The *kecak* is performed by around one hundred men who sit on the ground and then move simultaneously while calling 'cak-ke-cak-ke-cak'.

GAMELAN

A gamelan orchestra is made up of at least 30 musicians playing more than 70 instruments – mainly gongs, claves and metallophones, accompanied by flutes and string instruments. There is neither a melody nor are solos performed; the music acts as an accompaniment to dances or shadow theatre performances. The unusual tonality and frequent changes in rhythm can make it difficult for some tourists to get used to when they first hear it.

HINDUISM

Before the Javanese brought Hinduism to the island, the Balinese practiced animistic spirit worship and believed in a nature pervaded by the divine. Elements of this can still be found in the Balinese Hindu Dharma faith. According to this, the gods live in the mountains and the demons have their home in the sea. Not only in temples, but everywhere on the streets and in their houses, the Balinese make daily offerings to the gods and the demons. The supreme deity for Balinese Hindus is Sanghyang Widhi, in whom the three main gods Brahma, Vishnu and Shiva are embodied. Numerous minor deities live in the rivers, woods and other places.

Exotic to tourists' ears: gamelan music is played to entertain the gods

ISLAM

Almost 90 per cent of all Indonesians are followers of the Islam faith. Although only 10 per cent of Bali's population are Muslims, this is as high as 95 per cent on Lombok and the Gilis. Islam has become mixed with local traditions in west and central Lombok. Here, a sip of local palm wine is not considered a sin. However, it is even forbidden to drink beer in the strictly Islamic east of the island. Many Sasak people in the north of Lombok still adhere to *Wetu Telu* ('three elements'), a conglomeration of Islam, animistic and Hindu elements. Wetu Telu followers only pray three times a day and also fast for only three days. However, due to persecution in the past, very few openly profess their faith.

KITES

When the Balinese fly a kite it – like almost everything else here – has a spiritual significance: it is said that the god Indra liked play this sport himself. Half of the village is involved in building the kites that can be up to 8m (26ft) long with a tail measuring as much as another 12m (39ft). Around 1500 villages compete against each other at the annual Kite Festival in Sanur (July/August). Accompanied by a priest and gamelan music, as many as a dozen men are needed to get the work of art airborne.

KRETEK

Travellers to Indonesia will be greeted at the airport by the sweetish aroma of *kretek* cigarettes. In 1880, the Javanese Haji Jamahri mixed cloves with tobacco to soothe his asthma: cloves are considered a household remedy for pain relief. This resulted in one of Indonesia's largest industries; 95 per cent of the world's supply of cloves is used in the manufacture of *kretek*.

KUTA COWBOYS

A suntanned body, long hair and a cheeky grin are their trademarks: the Bali beach boys are always ready, willing and able to be of help to female tourists. Some of them are happy to be a companion for the holiday – often in the hope that it will lead to a lengthier relationship that will bring them financial benefits. The 2010 documentary 'Cowboys in Paradise' gives a detailed description of the background to this indirect form of sexual tourism – much to the annoyance of the Balinese officials. Although most of the beach boys are just harmless show-offs, it is a good idea to be careful.

PAINTING

Before colonisation, Bali paintings exclusively depicted Hindu myths. A sense of perspective was unknown in the so-called *Wayang* style and colours were only used a fillers. These kinds of pictures are still produced in the village of Kemasan near Klungkung. In the 1920s, the German Walter Spies and Dutchman Rudolf Bonnet, under the patronage of Prince Cokorda Gede Agung Sukawati, created the Pita Maha school of painting in Ubud. The Europeans introduced modern materials and techniques, but at the same time learnt the traditional art of the Balinese. The Dutchman Arie Smit started the Young Artist school of painting in Penestanan near Ubud in the 1960s. The artists' paintings are characterised by scenes of everyday life in strongly contrasting colours.

PANCASILA

The Sanskrit word *pancasila* means 'five principles' and has formed the foundation of the Indonesian state since independence. It is represented in the country's coat of arms above the motto 'Unity in Diversity'. The star stands for the belief in a Supreme Being (regardless of religion), the chain for humanity while the banyan tree represents national unity, the buffalo's head, democracy and the rice and cotton plants, social justice. However, in the past, the varying interpretations of

RICE CULTIVATION

Rice is a staple food in Indonesia. However, for the Balinese, it is not simply a plant but a symbol of the goddess of fertility Dewi Sri, who is worshiped in shrines in the fields. The rice fields are irrigated

The ritual temple dances demand the utmost control from the performers

the principle of religion have frequently produced political problems.

PUPUTAN

Rather die, than subjugate oneself: the entire court of the Prince of Bandung, dressed in their finest attire, confronted the Dutch army that had conquered Denpasar on 20 September 1906. Armed only with daggers, the men, women and children ran straight into the volley of gunfire of the invaders. Those who did not die in the battle then committed suicide in front of the horrified conquerors. This ritual mass suicide, known as *puputan,* was also committed by the royal Klungkung court in 1908.

by means of a complex canal system that is strictly controlled by farmer cooperatives *(subak)*. This democratic cultivation system, which is in tune with nature, was recognised by the UNESCO as part of the World's Cultural Heritage in 2012. Rice growing is a man's work, but three times a year the whole family helps harvest the crop. On Bali, the picturesque rice terraces cover the fertile volcanic slopes up to an altitude of over 1000m (3280ft).

TEMPLE

Balinese temples are walled compounds; the sky is considered the roof. The entrance is usually a split door guarded by stone demons. The interior of the temple consists of three courtyards with the third – and holiest – facing the mountains. This is where the holy shrines with their multi-tiered roofs are located. Each village has three temples: the *pura puseh* (origin temple) dedicated to Brahma the god of creation. The *pura desa* (village temple) is protected by Vishnu, the preserver, and is the centre of community life. The most rarely visited is the *pura dalem* (temple of the dead) consecrated to Shiva the god of destruction. The most important temple on Bali is the Pura Besakih on the Gunung Agung. It is one of the six most sacred temples, the *sad kahyangan*, that are also known as the 'Great State Temples' or 'Temples of the World', and are built at places of great importance. The other five are the Pura Lempuyang Luhur, Pura Goa Lawah, Pura Uluwatu, Pura Batukaru and Pura Pusering Jagat.

VILLAGE LIFE

Most Balinese live in village communities where everyone has specific obligations to fulfil – but is also given help whenever it is needed. Communal life is regulated by the traditional customary law *(adat)*. The public assembly *(banjar)*, which all married men belong to, decides on all important matters. This community spirit is also reflected in the layout of the village *(desa)*: there is a square *(alun alun)* with a large banyan tree, which is considered sacred, in the centre with the assembly hall and village temple – and frequently a music pavilion and cockfight arena – grouped around it. The centre of everyday life is the market *(pasar)*. The elected leaders of these traditional village communities also have great influence at the province level.

WALLACE LINE

In the 19th century, the British naturalist Sir Alfred Wallace discovered that the flora and fauna on the islands eastern part of Bali differed significantly from the rest of Asia. From this, he concluded that the border line between the Asian and Australian primeval continent formerly ran through the strait between Bali and Lombok: while monkeys, elephants and tigers live in the tropical rainforests to the west, the east is characterised by lizards, marsupials and dry savannah landscapes.

WAYANG KULIT

Indonesians had shadow theatres even before Hinduism conquered the islands: it was believed that the shadows could contact the spirits of dead ancestors. A puppeteer *(dalang)* sits in front of a screen with an oil lamp and makes the elaborate figures, embossed on buffalo skin, dance on their bamboo sticks. In catchy singsong, he recounts episodes from the epics *Ramayana* and *Mahabharata*. The gamelan plays in the background. A performance can last all night long; the spectators come and go, eat and chatter away, as they please.

WELLNESS

Bali is frequently called 'Asia's spa centre' – and, rightly so: it would be hard to beat the number and diversity of the spa services available on the island. Balinese, Javanese and Shiatsu massages, aromatherapy, body scrubs and treatments with hot stones are available in every hotel and offered on many street corners. The prices range from dirt cheap to almost unaffordable. An expensive massage does not necessarily mean that it is an excellent one; you often have to pay for the exotic atmosphere and stylish spa interiors. In any case, it is usually a good idea to look for a little more comfort than that offered by a cheap rubdown on the beach.

FOOD & DRINK

Spicy coconut curries, delicate meat skewers, crispy chicken and sophisticated fish dishes – the cooking in Bali and Lombok is fiery and full of variety. Rice is always served as an accompaniment – no meal would be complete without it: the Indonesians believe that a person who has not eaten any rice cannot possible be satisfied.

Every morning, the women in the household cook rice and several other dishes for their family. Having a meal together is not usual in everyday Indonesian life; everybody eats when they are hungry. This means that, in general, the food is lukewarm or cold – and that is how it is

also served in many restaurants. People eat with their fingers or with a spoon and fork. Chopsticks are only used for Chinese dishes such as *mie bakso* (noodle soup with meatballs) or *cap cay* (vegetables sautéed in soy sauce).

However all this changes on feast days: the men take over everything from slaughtering ducks and pigs to grinding the spice pastes when the ritual dishes are prepared for Balinese ceremonies. The work often takes days and cooking and eating become a shared social experience.

The spice pastes used give each dish its own special flavour. The various ingredients are pounded in a stone trough and

Photo: Satay skewers with rice

Turmeric, coconut, lemon grass – the food on Bali, Lombok and the Gilis is varied and, above all, always fresh

usually roasted for a short time. Ginger, turmeric, galangal and coriander are absolutely essential. Lemon grass, limes, salam leaves and tamarind add a touch of freshness to the spice mixture and palm sugar and kemiri nuts contribute a certain sweetness. This is all made complete with shrimp paste and chilli.

Most restaurants, which are usually open seven days a week, have long since adapt-ed their menus to cater to tourist tastes and serve milder variants of the Indonesian national dishes *nasi goreng* (fried rice), *mie goreng* (fried noodles), *gado-gado* (vegetable salad with peanut sauce) and *soto ayam* (chicken soup with lemon grass and turmeric) along with pizza, steak and sushi. These dishes are often accompanied by *satay* (small skewers of meat) or fried *tempe* (salty yeast cakes made with soya

LOCAL SPECIALITIES

▶ **ayam goreng** – crispy fried chicken
▶ **ayam taliwang** – crispy fried or grilled baby chicken with very spicy chilli sauce, from Lombok
▶ **babi guling** – suckling pig filled with spice paste, grilled over an open fire, a Balinese feast dish
▶ **balung nangka** – braised pork ribs with cooked jackfruit
▶ **bebek betutu** – duck stuffed with spice paste and then cooked for hours in banana leaves; Balinese feast dish
▶ **brem** – liquor made from the juice of the Aren palm
▶ **bubuh injin/bubur ketan hitam** – pudding of black sticky rice
▶ **ceramcam** – clear soup with young papaya and fish, chicken or pork
▶ **gado-gado** – vegetable salad with egg and tofu in peanut sauce
▶ **keupat cantok** – rice cooked in small packets of woven palm leaves, with vegetables and peanut sauce
▶ **kue lak-lak** – small round rice flour cakes with palm sugar and grated coconut
▶ **lawar** – minced meat with spice paste, jackfruit, young papaya, green beans and coconut
▶ **lontong** – rice cooked in banana leaves

▶ **mie goreng** – fried noodles, usually served with egg and cucumber (photo left)
▶ **nasi goreng** – fried rice, usually served with egg, krupuk and some salad (photo right)
▶ **nasi kuning** – festive rice, coloured yellow with turmeric and cooked in coconut milk
▶ **nasi rames** – rice dish with a variety of specialities to sample
▶ **pelecing kangkung** – water spinach with soy sprouts and spicy chilli tomato sauce
▶ **pelecingan** – chicken or fish fried or braised in very hot chilli paste, popular on Lombok
▶ **pepesan ikan** – fish steamed with spices in a banana leaf
▶ **sate ayam/babi/kambing** – small skewers with chicken, pork or goat meat, served with peanut or soy sauce
▶ **sate lilit** – chopped fish or seafood, mixed with coconut and spices and then grilled on small bamboo skewers
▶ **tuak** – wine from the juice of the Aren palm
▶ **urap-urap** – vegetable salad with a dressing of grated coconut, red onions, garlic, salt and chilli

sprouts), *sambal* (chilli dip) and *krupuk* (prawn crackers).

The food served in the *kaki lima* (mobile food carts) and *warungs* (street restaurants) is usually more authentic and often much tastier. In contrast to regular restaurants that usually do not take any orders after 10pm, they can be found open any time of day or night. However, you should only eat food that has been freshly cooked, fried or grilled. You should avoid food that has been standing uncovered for any length of time – the same applies to water that has not been boiled, ice cubes and sliced fruit (however, you can trust the ice cream and fruit served in the better restaurants). As a rule: if a *warung* is busy then the food is usually good.

In recent years, an increasing number of *rumah makan* (simple inns) and restaurant owners have rediscovered the value of their traditional cuisine and now have a wider selection of local specialities on their menus, but elaborate festive meals, such as *babi guling* (suckling pig) and *bebek betutu* (steamed duck), usually have to be ordered in advance.

Desserts are rather uncommon but there is a variety of cakes and puddings made of coconut or sticky rice. *Pisang goreng* (bananas fried in batter) is a popular snack. The choice of fruit is absolutely overwhelming: there are sweet mangos and papayas, rambutans, fragrant mangosteens, snake fruit, gigantic jackfruit, tart soursop and – in the eyes of the Indonesians – the queen of all fruits: the spiky durian, whose pungent smell has been known to make the stomach of many tourists churn.

This is served with tea or coffee that is made in the cup like mocha. If you don't say something beforehand, you will get it sugary sweet – and, if you order milk, be sure to say you don't mean sticky canned condensed milk *(susu kental)*. However, many cafés have now started making

Exotic fruits are turned into refreshing drinks

caffè latte and the like, although most of the hotels still serve Nescafé at breakfast. The fruit juices are a real highlight: blended with crushed ice and a dash of milk or lime juice, pineapple, melon, guava and avocado become a special treat. Beer is available everywhere and *Storm Beer* (brewed on Bali according to German and English recipes) is especially recommended. Wine lovers will have to dig deeper into their pockets; the most inexpensive are the *Hatten* wines produced on Bali. In contrast to Muslim Lombok, there is a wide range of strong spirits on Bali – from self-distilled liqueurs to potent *arak* (rice liquor). But beware: stay well away from those self-distilled liqueurs! Adulterated alcohol has already led to several cases of severe methanol poisoning on Bali and Lombok. If your stomach plays up after all of these unaccustomed foods, it is a good idea to reach for a *kelapa muda* (young coconut): its water is not only refreshing but is also said to have curative powers.

Online restaurant guides for Bali: *www.balieats.com, www.bali-resto.com*.

SHOPPING

Bali is a shopper's paradise – clothing, arts and crafts, and jewellery are available in every price range. Indonesians come from across the country to the arts and crafts market in Sukawati, 20km (12mi) north of Sanur. This is where useful and decorative items from Bali, Lombok and Java are sold. Lombok is famous for its woven fabrics and ceramics. The most inexpensive places to buy these are where they are made or at the market – but there, you will have to bargain. As a rule of thumb: take off at least 50 per cent of the first price asked. If you are planning on making a lot of purchases then get up early: the traders believe that a day's success depends on the first sale and they often offer lower prices in the morning. The shops in the tourist centres usually have fixed prices but they are more expensive. Beware of buying antiques – very few of them are really old.

CARVINGS

Mythical figures, masks, stylised fruit or complete door frames: the Balinese carve just about everything. The wood carvers in the village of Mas near Ubud are real masters of their art.

CERAMICS

Pejaten on Bali is famous for its colourful, elaborately decorated ceramics. However, most of the pottery comes from Lombok: the Sasak in Banyumulek and Masbagik produce simple, elegant terracotta goods.

FABRICS

Almost all of the classic batik fabrics come from Java but the Balinese have adapted the technique and created their own motifs. Good quality is recognisable if the patterns are equally distinct on both sides of the fabric. *Ikat* woven fabrics are typical of Bali and Lombok, they can take weeks or even months to make. With *ikat* you should pay particular attention to the quality of the colours. *Geringsing* fabrics from the Bali Aga village of Tenganan are very special: the fabric is considered sacred and only a few women are still able to produce these extremely rare fabrics. The double-sided patterns are created using the

Colourful fabrics, shadow puppets, pearl necklaces and wickerwork – the souvenirs on Bali, Lombok and the Gilis are plentiful

highly complicated double ikat process and can cost millions of rupiah.

JEWELLERY

There are good silver and goldsmiths on Bali. The most famous village is Celuk near Ubud but it is unfortunately overrun by tourist buses. **INSIDER TIP** Beautiful champagne-coloured pearls come from Lombok but there are also glistening black and pink pearls imported from Tahiti and China respectively. The coloured semi-precious stones usually come from Kalimantan. If you are interested in good quality, buy only in recommended shops.

KRIS

These ornate daggers are essential items at dances and ceremonies and are impor-tant for the status of a man who inherits

his father's weapon. High-quality *kris* are available in good antique shops; cheaper versions can be bought in the silversmiths' village of Celuk near Ubud.

WAYANG

Beautiful shadow theatre puppets *(wayang kulit)* are expensive; they are notable for the pattern of the pressing in buffalo leather. Only if they show signs of having been used can you be sure that they are old. The same applies to the wooden marionettes *(wayang golek)*; most come from West Java.

WICKERWORK

Baskets, boxes, bags and coasters made of bamboo, palm leaves or rattan are perfect gifts to take home; they can be put to many uses and are light.

THE PERFECT ROUTE

NIGHTLIFE, SHOPPING, SURFING

① *Seminyak* → p. 61 is the ideal place to arrive in Bali. Get over your jetlag with a stroll through the chic boutiques and cafés and enjoy your first sunset drink in the legendary Ku Dé Ta beach club. On the next day, make a moped excursion to the Bukit Peninsula and visit the **②** *Pura Luhur Uluwatu Temple* → p. 38 at its spectacular location. A small road leads from there to Suluban and Padang-Padang bays where you will be able to watch the best surfers on the island in action. On your way back, you should make a stop in **③** *Kuta's* → p. 44 souvenir quarter and later try out the nightclub scene at the Double Six Beach in Legian.

CULTURE AND WELLNESS

On the third day, take the Perama shuttle bus *(www.peramatour. com)* to **④** *Ubud* → p. 66, Bali's cultural and wellness centre. A walk to the Sari Organik (a farm where you will be able to taste delicious organic dishes surrounded by rice fields) continues on a circular route until you reach the Ubud Sari Health Resort that offers massages. In the evening, watch a dance performance after you have visited the Puri Lukisan (photo left). Next morning, get on your bicycle and head towards the holy cave Goa Gajah and then on to the old royal city **⑤** *Pejeng* → p. 73 and further to Tampaksiring with the Gunung Kawi burial site and the sacred springs **⑥** *Tirta Empul* → p. 73.

VOLCANOES AND RICE TERRACES

On the next day, hire a car with a driver for your excursion to Penelokan. From there, you will have the best views of the active volcano, the **⑦** *Gunung Batur* → p. 72. You should schedule an extra day if you want to hike to its summit. Next you drive over mountain roads until you reach **⑧** *Pura Besakih* → p. 41, the most sacred temple on Bali, high up on the slopes of the Gunung Agung, and continue on to Sidemen with fantastic views over the verdant rice terraces. You should take a look at the old court hall Kerta Gosa in **⑨** *Klungkung* → p. 54 before treating yourself to a night in the elegant Alila Manggis Hotel.

OFF TO THE ISLANDS

Take a taxi to **⑩** *Padang Bai* → p. 53 (photo right) the next morning;

the speedboats for the Gilis depart from there (book in good time!). **11** *Gili Meno* → p. 94 is the most unspoilt of the three islands and a wonderful place to relax. Hire a boat complete with snorkelling or diving equipment: the skippers know where the most beautiful corals and sea turtles are to be found. After sunset, set sail for the party island **12** *Gili Trawangan* → p. 95 and dive into the exuberant nightlife.

HANDICRAFT AND TRADITION

The route continues by boat to Teluk Nare where you can visit the **13** *Autore Pearl Farm* → p. 87. Hop on to one of the minibuses *(bemo)* that drive along the picturesque coastal road from Bangsal to **14** *Senggigi* → p. 86. Here you can enjoy the relaxed atmosphere on the beach and an excellent dinner. On the following day, have your driver take you to the **15** *Pura Lingsar* → p. 81 temple complex and **16** *Taman Narmada* → p. 82. Then head to **17** *Banyumulek and Sukarara* → p. 89 on your way to the **18** *Sasak villages of Rambitan and Sade* → p. 79.

BEAUTIFUL BEACHES ON THE INDIAN OCEAN

Spend the night in the Sempiak Villas on the stunning beach at **19** *Selong Belanak* → p. 78 and then explore the other hidden coves and secluded beaches around **20** *Kuta* → p. 76 by boat or moped before allowing yourself one last ride surf, snorkel or dive in Mawun, Gerupuk or **21** *Ekas Bay* → p. 79 before heading back to the airport.

450km (280mi). Travel time: 17 hours
Recommended duration: 12 days
A detailed map of the route can be found on the back cover, in the road atlas and on the pull-out map

BALI

Most visitors are overwhelmed by the many exotic impressions that meet them on arrival in Bali: one moment they are in the midst of the chaotic traffic – with cars honking their horns and moped zigzagging between them – and then, just a few moments later, in the fragrant world of frangipani blossoms, soothing gamelan music and mystical temple ceremonies that dominate the everyday life of the Balinese.

Each family – and every hotel – pays tribute several times a day to their house gods with offerings of fruit, rice, flowers and incense. Dressed in sarongs, with sashes and headdresses, the staff and shop owners place their gifts in intricately woven palm-leaf baskets on the small altars. Even more impressive are the spectacular holiday processions, when an entire village makes its way – everybody in their finest clothes accompanied by the sound of loud gongs – to the temple, with the women balancing elaborate pyramids of fruit and other offerings on their heads. Bali is an enclave in the country with world's largest Muslim population: 93 per cent of the island's around 4 million inhabitants are Hindus. As a result of their late colonisation and early tourist development, the Balinese were able to preserve their unique culture. Their view of

Photo: Tirtagangga

Volcanoes and coral reefs, nightclubs and idyllic beaches, shrines and spas – Bali's many facets will surprise you

the world is formed by their own mythology in which the sea is peopled by demons and the gods live in the mountains. Their most sacred temple, the Pura Besakih, is located on the slopes of the 3148m (10,328ft) high Gunung Agung volcano, the highest – and holiest – mountain on Bali. Raging rivers flow through the deep gorges, lush forests and picturesque rice terraces run down to the beaches of white sand in the south and volcanic black in the north. Each Balinese spends about a third of his time carrying out his traditional obligations to the gods and the community. In Bali, the administration and sections of jurisdiction are still completely in the hands of the village communities, the *banjar,* which every married man belongs to. However, many Balinese are finding it increasingly difficult to balance their

The Balinese welcome the New Year with demon figures made out of bamboo and papier-mâché

traditions with modern life. Globalisation has impacted on the small Indonesian island: the around 3 million international tourists from not only bring foreign currency, but also a great number of influences from abroad, with them to the 2200 square mile island. This can be felt most strongly in Kuta where the majority of the visitors are chiefly interested in sun, sea, surfing and partying. There is a string of restaurants, bars and hotels all the way to chic Seminyak 4km (2.5mi) to the north. In the 1970s, the tourist resort Nusa Dua was established on the beaches on the Bukit Peninsula in the south in an attempt to prevent the masses of holidaymakers overrunning the whole island – today, this is a segregated world of hotel complexes.

Tourists who want to get away from the hustle and bustle to relax, snorkel or dive will find what they are looking for in the north and east of the island in Amed, Lovina and Pemuteran. Ubud, on the other hand, is increasingly becoming a Mecca for visitors interested in cultural and religion. A growing number of companies are therefore geared towards a more elite tourism, with exclusive villas and eco-friendly activities – yoga courses and organic cuisine are de rigueur.

AMED

(133 E4) *(ⓜ N3)* **Rugged hills and small bays characterise the rough beauty of Bali's eastern coast.**

The stretch of the coast south of the fishing village of Amed was once particularly poor, that has since changed and it has developed into a haven for travellers who want to escape the crowded tourist centres: in the past ten years, hotels and restaurants have multiplied along the narrow coastal road that runs from Amed via

Jemeluk, Bunutan, Lipah and Selang to the south. In spite of this, Amed has remained extremely peaceful making it possible for families and dive enthusiasts to have a relaxing holiday there. Most of the – usually rather small – holiday places are either located high up on the cliffs or on the dark, sandy beaches that are ideal for bathing or snorkelling. At dusk you can watch the fisherman set out to sea in their colourful outrigger boats. There is little in the way of shopping or nightlife in Amed, but that makes a relaxed dinner by candlelight all the more romantic.

You can cross over to the Gilis from Amed (45 minutes; Kuda Hitam Express | www.kudahitamexpress.com or Gili Sea Express | www.gili-sea-express.com).

FOOD & DRINK

AIONA
Vegetarian restaurant with European and Ayurveda dishes, as well as meditation courses and spiritual counselling. Bunutan | tel. 0813 38 16 17 30 | Budget–Moderate

SAILS ᨑ
Fresh seafood, steaks and delicious desserts served on an airy terrace high above the sea. Lean Beach | tel. 0363 2 20 06 | Moderate

INSIDER TIP ▶ WAWA WEWE BEACH
The newest of the four branches of this family business offers simple but good Western and Indonesian cuisine and is a meeting place for locals and tourists who gather here to dance to live music twice a week. Amed | tel. 0363 2 35 22 | Budget

SPORTS & ACTIVITIES

Amed is particularly attractive for divers and snorkellers: you can set out on your underwater safari from most of the bays and be sure to find colourful corals and schools of fish – the best are in Jemeluk and Lipah. The reef off the coast at Jemeluk and the small island Gili Selang are very popular diving spots. There is a spectacular coral wall, as well as an American supply ship from the Second World War

★ Pura Luhur Uluwatu
Ancient temple on the cliffs on the south coast → p. 38

★ Tenganan
Experience the culture and traditions of Bali's indigenous population, the Bali Aga → p. 42

★ Seminyak
After shopping, sip a cocktail in one of Bali's trendiest beach bars and enjoy the sunset → p. 61

★ Danau Buyan and Tamblingan
Rice fields and waterfalls invite visitors to take an idyllic stroll → p. 50

★ Nusa Lembongan
Ideal for snorkelling, surfing or simply relaxing → p. 51

★ Pulau Menjangan
Dives in the middle of the Taman Nasional Bali Barat national park → p. 57

★ Gunung Batukaru
Lush rice terraces with a breathtaking panorama and a mystical temple in the woods → p. 64

★ Ubud
Discover the spiritual side of Bali through the art, spas and yoga of this holy place → p. 66

★ Gunung Batur
Bizarre volcanic landscape and ancient traditions → p. 72

MARCO POLO HIGHLIGHTS

that is covered with coral, somewhat further to the north off the coast at *Tulamben* – this is one of the main attractions for divers in Bali. In recent years, various international resorts with their own diving schools have opened their doors here. The journey from Amed only takes around half an hour, but it is even faster by boat. *Jukung Dive (Amed | tel. 0363 2 34 69 | www.jukungdivebali.com)* and *Eco Dive (Jemeluk | tel. 0363 2 34 82 | www.ecodivebali.com)* offer diving courses and tours and the *Titi Sedana Homestay (tel. 0877 62 02 37 11 | titisedana@yahoo. com)* organises trips out to sea on fishing boats.

WHERE TO STAY

BLUE MOON VILLAS ☆
Spacious bungalows on the steep slope at Selang; sea view from all the rooms, excellent restaurant, two pools and spa. *14 rooms | Selang | tel. 0363 2 14 28 | www. bluemoonvilla.com | Moderate*

INSIDER TIP THE KAMPUNG
Private accommodation in two traditional Javanese wooden houses with pool directly on the beach; cleaning and a private dining service. *5 rooms | Jl. Abang-Adem | Bunutan | tel. 0363 2 30 58 | www.the kampung.com | Moderate*

PALM GARDEN AMED BEACH & SPA RESORT
Bright, modern bungalow complex with pool, spa and restaurant directly on the beach; built according to feng shui principles. *11 bungalows | Lean Village | Bunutan | tel. 0828 97 69 18 50 | www. palmgardenamed.com | Expensive*

HOTEL UYAH AMED ☺
Eco-resort with solar energy that has two pools, a spa and restaurant, and is well integrated into the village. *27 bungalows | Amed | tel. 0363 2 34 62 | www.hoteluyah. com | Budget*

WHERE TO GO

AMLAPURA (133 E5) (*Ø N4*)
The old seat of the once-powerful Karangasem Kingdom is around 25km (16mi) south of Amed. Today it is a small district capital with a population of 40,000. However, it is still worth making a stopover to stroll through the narrow streets with their Chinese shops and Muslim *warungs* and visit the two royal palaces: the *Puri Agung (daily 8am–5pm | entrance fee 10,000 Rp)* in Dutch colonial style was a gift from the occupiers and, complete with its water pavilion, is still well preserved. The expansive 18th century complex of the *Puri Gede (daily 8am–5pm | entrance fee 10,000 Rp)* opposite it is rather dilapidated but there are some interesting pictures and insignias of power waiting to be discovered.

TIRTAGANGGA (133 D5) (*Ø N4*)
The sacred springs of Tirtagangga ('Holy Water of the Ganges'), around which the last King of Karangasem had a park laid out in 1948, are surrounded by rice terraces 18km (11mi) southwest of Amed. Several pools, with ornate waterspouts and statues, splash down over three levels in the luxuriant garden. It is possible to swim in the pools if you pay an extra fee *(10,000 Rp)*. *Daily 8am–6pm | entrance fee 10,000 Rp.*

UJUNG WATER PALACE (133 E5) (*Ø N4*)
The *Taman Soekasada Ujung (daily 8am–5pm | entrance fee 10,000 Rp)*, which the King of Karangasem had built as his family residence in 1921, lies 30km (19mi) south of Amed. It was severely damaged by an

earthquake in 1979 and the renovations that were carried out are a bit too modern; however, the pools and garden still attract visitors to take a stroll and admire the view of the Gunung Agung. A ✳ winding coastal road leads back to Amed from Ujung. If you decide that you want to enjoy the peaceful atmosphere a little longer, you can spend the night in one of the seven airy villas in the ● *Seraya Shores Resort (tel. 0813 37 15 34 44 | www.seraya shores.com | Moderate)* and enjoy the pool above ocean and a healthy table d'hôte meal that is made using the fresh ingredients the chef bought in the morning.

BUKIT PENINSULA

(134–135 B–D 5–6) (⑳ H–J 7–8) The Bukit Badung Peninsula – often simply called 'Bukit' (hill) – hangs like a droplet from the southern tip of Bali.
Previously, the extremely dry climate meant that the peninsula was hardly inhabited but today the – up to 200m (656ft) high – limestone cliffs have become famous as the 'millionaire mile'. In the past ten years, many luxurious resorts have opened high up on the spectacular cliffs and Kuta's club scene now also stretches this far. As early as in the 1970s, the government established the hotel city *Nusa Dua* on the eastern beach of the peninsula in an effort to better channel mass tourism. Three heavily guarded gates lead from the small harbour town of *Tanjung Benoa* into the isolated five-star world that offers tourists everything they want – except genuine Balinese life. A better place to observe that is in *Jimbaran* on the west coast where the colourful fishing boats come back in the morning and evening and sell their catch

Many roads lead to the Nusa Dua Hotel complex – this is one of them

to the row of the simple restaurants along the beach. The area is especially popular with surfers who come to enjoy the bays in the southwest.

SIGHTSEEING

MUSEUM PASIFIKA ●
This spacious museum in modern Balinese architectural style is in the middle of the

Nusa Dua hotel complex and not only has art from Indonesia but also from Europe, Indo-China, East Asia and the Pacific islands. *Daily 10am–6pm | entrance fee 70,000 Rp | Block P | Nusa Dua*

PURA LUHUR ULUWATU ★ ⚄

This 11th century temple, standing 80m (262ft) above the surf, was built to honour the goddess of the sea and is one of the six holiest temples in Bali. A staircase lined with frangipani trees leads to the outer courtyard of the temple whose curved door is guarded by figures of Ganesha.

Scenes from Balinese mythology are carved into the white coral walls. Only Hindus are permitted to enter the middle and inner courtyards. A narrow pathway leads through the temple area along the precipitous coast and has breathtaking views of the sea raging down below. It is especially recommended to visit at sunset when the *Kecak* dance is performed in front of the silhouette of the temple. However, be sure that your valuables, cameras and sunglasses are well hidden to protect them from being stolen by the brash monkeys. *Daily 9am–7pm, Kecak daily 6pm | entrance fee 15,000 Rp, Kecak 50,000 Rp.*

FOOD & DRINK

All of the luxury hotels in Nusa Dua and on the rest of the peninsula have excellent – expensive – restaurants. The *warungs* on the beach in Jimbaran are the best places to go for great – inexpensive – seafood.

BALIQUE RESTAURANT

Delicious fusion cuisine in airy, sophisticated vintage style architecture. *Jl. Uluwatu 39 | Jimbaran | tel. 0361 70 49 45 | Moderate–Expensive*

BUMBU BALI

Award-winning master chef Heinz von Holzen serves an exquisite selection of Balinese dishes, and also offers cooking courses. *Jl. Pratama | Tanjung Benoa | tel. 0361 77 22 99 | Moderate*

INSIDER TIP ▶ ROCK BAR ⚄

Ultra-chic bar in the Ayana Resort that has a spectacular setting on a rock 14m (46ft) above the sea and a fabulous panoramic view; all this accompanied by cocktails, snacks and international DJs. *Jl. Karang Mas Sejahtera | Jimbaran | tel. 0361 70 22 22 | Expensive*

TAO BALI

Modern Asian cuisine in chic lounge atmosphere. *Jl. Pratama 96 | Tanjung Benoa | tel. 0361 77 29 02 | Moderate*

SPORTS & ACTIVITIES

The large hotels offer all kinds of water sports, as well as tennis courts and luxurious spas. The spectacular waves, which attract surfers from all around the world, are the main attraction in the southwest of the peninsula. Courses can be booked from the *Padang Surf Camp (tel. 0819 99 28 35 49 | www.balisurfingcamp.com)*. Golfers will discover one of Asia's finest courses in the *Bali Golf and Country Club* in Nusa Dua. The *New Kuta Golf* in Pecatu with sea views *(information under www.99bali.com/golf)* is a good alternative.

BEACHES

The peninsula's most expansive beaches are in the *Nusa Dua* hotel complex. Major sections of the beach at *Tanjung Benoa*, as well as in the south of *Jimbaran*, have also been taken over by hotels. The long strip in front of the fish w*arungs* in Jimbaran is more suitable for going for a walk. The very attractive *Dreamland Beach* is unfortunately almost always crowded and rather built up. *Bingin, Balangan* and *Padang-Padang* are three bays that are very popular with surfers and where swimming and snorkelling is also possible but they are somewhat more difficult to reach. However, non-surfers and beginners are well advised to just look at the breakers at Impossibles, Nyang-Nyang, Suluban and Uluwatu.

WHERE TO STAY

BALI BULE HOMESTAY
The beautiful family hotel, with pool and restaurant, is only a five-minute drive away from Suluban and Padang-Padang. Ideal for surfers. *10 rooms | Jl. Pantai Padang-Padang | Pecatu | tel. 0361 76 99 79 | balibulehomestay.com | Budget*

BALI REEF RESORT
Well maintained bungalow resort with pool, spa and beach restaurant – particularly suitable for families. *28 rooms | Jl.*

Pratama | Tanjung Benoa | tel. 0361 77 62 91 | www.balireef-resort.com | Expensive

JIMBARAN PURI BALI
Chic, designer resort set in a spacious tropical garden, gigantic pool, spa, restaurant and bar directly on the beach; special offers for families and wedding service. *64 cottages | Jl. Uluwatu | Jimbaran | tel. 0361 70 16 05 | www.jimbaranpuribali. com | Expensive*

INSIDER TIP THE TEMPLE LODGE ☼ ☺
Spend the night in one of the seven individually decorated suites on the rocks above Bingin and enjoy fresh organic cuisine, a pool and a spa that uses natural products. Daily yoga classes. *Jl. Pantai | Bingin | tel. 0857 39 01 15 72 | www.the templelodge.com | Moderate*

UDAYANA KINGFISHER ECO LODGE ☼ ☺
Located on a hill in the middle of the campus of the Udayana University this hotel offers a well-planned ecological concept

Fun on the beach between corals and limestone cliffs on Bukit Peninsula

with a peaceful and natural environment far away from the beaten tourist track. *10 rooms, 2 villas for longer stays | Kampus Udayana | Jimbaran | tel. 0361 74 74 2 05 | www.ecolodgesindonesia.com | Moderate*

CANDIDASA

(133 D6) *(∅ N5)* **This former fishing village (pop. 20,000) that is often described as the 'old Bali' has managed to retain its original charm although this is not always apparent at first sight.**
During the tourism boom in the 1970s, the coral reefs off the coast were plundered to provide building material – and, a decade later, the surf had completely destroyed the beach. Today, ugly concrete walls protect the main town from further erosion. However, there are bungalows in palm groves and beautiful beaches to the east and west of the centre. Candidasa is an ideal starting point for excursions into Bali's mountainous eastern region.

FOOD & DRINK

CANDI BAKERY
Small German café with a `INSIDER TIP` pleasant homestay *(Budget)*. This is the place to go to for delicious whole-wheat bread and fresh pastries and imported beer. *Jl. Tenganan | Ds. Nyuhte bel 7 | tel. 0363 41883 | Budget*

JOGLO BAR & RESTAURANT
International and original dishes from Bali and Java are served in a traditional Javanese *joglo* house. *Jl. Raya Candidasa (next to Indomaret) | tel. 0363 42181 | www.joglocandidasa.com | Moderate*

VINCENT'S
Homely restaurant and bar with international cooking and a good selection of cocktails and wine; live jazz. *Jl. Raya Candidasa | tel. 0363 41368 | www.vincentsbali.com | Moderate*

BEACHES

The beach directly to the east of the main road in Candidasa is rather narrow but the sands widen the further one travels westwards. The unspoiled *Pasir Putih* ('White Sand') beach is very popular: a bumpy road starting about 5km (3mi) northeast of Candidasa leads to a sandy beach surrounded by rocks with crystal-clear water. Very crowded after midday.

WHERE TO STAY

ALILA MANGGIS ☺
Elegant hotel complex under coconut palms on the lovely beach to the west of Candidasa. Pool, spa, yoga classes and exquisite restaurant. The eco-conscious management has initiated a waste recycling project in the nearby village. *55 rooms | Buitan Manggis | tel. 0363 41011 | www.alilahotels.com | Expensive*

RAMASHINTA HOTEL
Charming hotel set in a garden with a view of the sea, pool and restaurant on the lagoon in the centre of Candidasa. *15 rooms | Jl. Raya Candidasa | Dusun Samuh | tel. 0363 41903 | www.ramashintahotel.com | Moderate*

`INSIDER TIP` SEA BREEZE
This well maintained complex on the beach at Mendira has a restaurant with a relaxed atmosphere, two pools and a spa. *Mendira | tel. 0812 108 58 88 | www.seabreezecandidasa.com | Moderate*

THE WATERGARDEN ⚘
The hotel's 13 bungalows are hidden between rippling lotus ponds in a lush garden

on a slope. Two pools, spa and restaurant. *Jl. Raya Candidasa | tel. 0363 41540 | www.watergardenhotel.com | Expensive*

WHERE TO GO

GUNUNG AGUNG
(132–133 C–D 3–4) (*M–N 3–4*)

According to Balinese beliefs, the gods live on the summit of the majestic – usually cloud-capped – 'Great Mountain'

PURA BESAKIH ⚜
(132 C4) (*L–M4*)

Bali's largest and most important temple, the 'Mother Temple', is around 40km (25mi) northwest of Candidasa. At an altitude of around 1000m (3289ft) on the slopes of the Gunung Agung, it offers stunning views. Its origins date back to the 11th century and today it consists of 22 temples at various heights on the mountain slopes. The symbolic centre is

The morning mist veils the central temple complex of the Pura Besakih

(3148m/10,328ft). They showed their displeasure in 1963 when the last eruption of the volcano destroyed large areas of eastern Bali. The strenuous climb up to the 700m (2297ft) wide crater can be made from *Besakih (around 6 hours for experienced mountaineers)* or from *Pura Pasar Agung (around 4 hours)*. A guide is not obligatory but recommendable.

formed by the *Pura Penataran Agung* with a lotus throne dedicated to the god Shiva. It is only worth visiting Pura Besakih with a knowledgeable guide because the long path from the car park to the temple complex has developed into a tourist trap with dozens of intrusive so-called guides and vendors pestering the visitors. *Daily 8am–6pm | entrance fee 15,000 Rp.*

Traditional dwelling in the
Bali Aga village of Tenangan

TENGANAN ★ (133 D5) (🗺 N4–5)

The Bali Aga, the indigenous population of Bali, live a strictly traditional life in a few secluded villages. Tenganan, 3km (2mi) north of Candidasa, is the only Bali Aga village that is open to tourism. The traditional houses go way up the hill to the left and right of the village square. Visitors who make a donation can take a look inside and watch the people living there making basketwork, manuscripts from the leaves of the lontar palm and the famous *Geringsing* fabrics: only a few women still master the art of producing an *ikat* cloth that is woven on both sides. Creating these expensive fabrics, which are said to have magic powers, can take several years. The young men of the village fight each other with pandanus leaves at the annual *Usaba Sambah Festival* in June.

DENPASAR

(134–135 C–D4) (🗺 J6–7) **Bali's capital city is characterised by modern commercial centres, administration buildings and more than enough traffic. The 700,000 inhabitants come from all parts of the country and the vibrant life reflects Indonesian reality.**

In the southwest Denpasar flows almost seamlessly into Seminyak, in the southeast the suburbs stretch as far as Sanur. Most tourists just pass through Denpasar, but the former royal city – which was earlier known as *Badung* – has many buildings and parks that are well worth visiting, as well as a historical museum and culture centre. The old royal palace was almost completely destroyed at the time of the Dutch conquest in 1906 and today only the small palaces *Puri Satria (Jl. Veteran)*, *Puri Pemecutan (Jl. Thamrin)* and *Puri Jero Kuta (Jl. Dr. Sutomo)* can be seen. Although the colonial rulers established the seat of their administration in Singaraja, Denpasar had already become an important trading centre in the 1930s – however, it did not achieve its status as Bali's capital city until 1958.

> **CITY** **WHERE TO START?**
> **Jl. Gajah Mada:** Denpasar's main thoroughfare starts south of the bus terminus in the west, where all the intercity buses arrive, and cuts straight through the centre. This is also the site of the two markets, the Pasar Badung and Pasar Kumbasari. If you follow the street a few hundred yards to the west you reach Puputan Square with the Pura Jagatnatha and the Bali Museum.

SIGHTSEEING

TAMAN WEDHI BUDAYA (ARTS CENTRE)
The cultural centre is located in a park in the eastern section of Denpasar. The spacious complex includes the art academy, a gallery and three open-air stages. It gets really crowded during the *Bali Arts Festival (www.baliartsfestival.com)* that is held every year in June/July. *Mon–Thu, Sat 8am–2.30pm, Fri 8am–12.30pm | Jl. Nusa Indah*

BALI MUSEUM (MUSEUM NEGERI PROPINSI BALI)
The Bali Provincial Public Museum exhibits prehistoric artefacts, dance costumes, religious objects and gamelan instruments. Today, the museum, which was founded by the Dutch in 1910, is made up of four buildings in Balinese palace and temple architecture from various epochs including the period of the Gelgel and Karangasem dynasties. ● Children's dance groups train in the inner courtyard every Saturday at 4pm *(free admission)*. *Sat–Thu 8am–4pm, Fri 8.30am–12.30pm | entrance fee 10,000 Rp | Jl. Mayor Wisnu*

PUPUTAN SQUARE
A memorial on the green square in the centre of Denpasar commemorates the ritual suicides *(puputan)* of the Princes of Badung and Tabanan, who defied the Dutch – unarmed – together with their entire courts in 1906 in order to evade colonisation. Those who were not slaughtered in the volleys of gunfire killed themselves after the massacre. Today, the square is a popular after work meeting place.

PURA JAGATNATHA
Located on the eastern side of Puputan Square is Bali's state temple. It was built in 1953 and is dedicated to the supreme deity Sanghyang Widhi who unites Shiva, Brahma and Vishnu in one entity and in this way satisfies the Indonesian national philosophy of *pancasila* (monotheism). The shrine is made of white coral. There are *wayang* performances on full moon nights when the Balinese philosophise, drink and flirt in front of the temple.

FOOD & DRINK

INSIDER TIP ▶ BHINEKA JAYA CAFE
The café run by Bali's best-known coffee producer is actually a colonial era warehouse. It serves coffee roasted in-house, including Kopi Luwak, the world's most expensive variety. *Jl. Gajah Mada | www.kopibali.com*

The Pura Jagatnatha temple is one of the most important holy places on Bali

PASAR MALAM KERENENG
The lively night market has stalls offering dishes from all over Indonesia. *Jl. Kamboja | Budget*

SHOPPING

Along with modern shopping malls, Denpasar has several interesting markets: the largest is the *Pasar Badung (Jl. Gajah Mada)* where fresh food can already be bought from 5 o'clock in the morning. The *Pasar Kumbasari* on the other side of the river is the place to go for arts and crafts and souvenirs. The bird market, *Pasar Burung (Jl. Veteran),* is very colourful but not for the faint of heart; not only feathered creatures, but also other small animals and insects are sold there.

WHERE TO STAY

INNA BALI
Denpasar's oldest international hotel, which was built by the Dutch in 1927, still exudes a colonial atmosphere. Restaurant and swimming pool. *71 rooms | Jl. Veteran-hotel 3 | tel. 0361 22 56 81 | www.innabali. com | Budget–Moderate*

INFORMATION

DENPASAR GOVERNMENT TOURISM OFFICE
Jl. Surapati 7 | tel. 0361 23 45 69 | www.balidenpasartourism.com

KUTA/LEGIAN

MAP INSIDE BACK COVER
(134 C4–5) (*ℳ H–J7*) Before the hippies and surfers discovered the mile long beach (with endless rolling waves) in the 1960s, Kuta was a simple fishing village with unpaved roads.

The only traces of the old village left in what has become Bali's most important tourist centre (pop. 40,000) are the narrow streets around Poppies Lane. There is an unending press of cars, mopeds and hawkers along the seaside promenade and *Jalan Legian* that links Kuta and Legian. Countless hotels, restaurants and shops are lined up next to each other and the borders to the neighbouring towns of Tuban in the south and Seminyak in the north have ceased to exist: Kuta and Legian have amalgamated to become an urban conglomerate that has now reached the limits of its growth. But it is precisely this pulsating density that is so attractive to surfers and party fans who want to enjoy the sea, sun and the surf during the day and the nightlife after dark. In contrast, somewhat more peaceful Tuban offers everything visitors need for a family holiday from an amusement park to shopping mall.

Kuta has also recovered from the shock of the bombings in 2002 and 2005 when more than 200 people lost their lives. The Balinese authorities have increased security measures and tourists are now returning for their holidays. A memorial at the site of one of the nightclubs commemorates the victims.

FOOD & DRINK

THE BALCONY ⚜
(U B4) (*ℳ b4*)
Popular meeting place for surfers, with a wide variety of Western and Asian dishes. *Jl. Benesari 16 | Kuta | tel. 0361 75 06 55 | Moderate*

ENVY ⚜ (U A5) (*ℳ a5*)
The friendly staff in this hip beach lounge serve delicious pasta, steaks, seafood and cocktails. *Jl. Wana Segara 33 | Tuban | tel. 0361 75 25 27 | Moderate–Expensive*

You will be able to find traditional accessories on Kuta's shopping streets

INSIDER TIP KORI RESTAURANT & BAR
(U B4) (𝄞 b4)
A peaceful oasis in the heart of Kuta: enjoy the Balinese specialities and international cuisine in a beautiful garden. Cigar and cognac lounge. *Poppies Lane II | Kuta | tel. 0361 75 86 05 | Moderate*

MADE'S WARUNG I AND II
Always full, the cheerful staff pamper the guests with a great variety of tasty Indonesian food. *Jl. Pantai Kuta* (U B5) (𝄞 b5) *and Jl. Raya Seminyak* (U B3) (𝄞 b3) *| tel. 0286 2 17 10 45 | Moderate*

NERO BALI MEDITERRANEAN RESTAURANT & LOUNGE (U B4) (𝄞 b4)
Mediterranean cuisine and an excellent wine list, complemented by delicious desserts and coffees. *Jl. Legian Kelod 384 | Legian | tel. 0361 75 07 56 | Moderate–Expensive*

TEKOR BALI (U B3) (𝄞 b3)
Beach restaurant with laid-back atmosphere and good international cuisine. *Jl. Arjuna 99 | Legian Kaja | tel. 0361 73 52 68 | Budget–Moderate*

SHOPPING

BIN HOUSE
The wearable Indonesian fashions are handmade using exquisite fabrics and traditional styles. *Discovery Shopping Mall MG 30 | Jl. Kartika Plaza* (U B5) (𝄞 b5) *| Kuta and Made's Warung | Jl. Raya Seminyak* (U B3) (𝄞 b3) *| Seminyak | www.binhouse.com*

CELLARDOOR ● (U 0) (𝄞 0)
Bali's Hatten Wines shop not only sells their own wines but also those produced by the Dewi Sri distillery, and there are daily wine tastings. *Komplex Pertokoan Dewa Ruci 3, Bypass Ngurah Rai | tel. 0361 76 74 22 | www.hattenwines.com*

DISCOVERY SHOPPING MALL ●
(U B5) (𝄞 b5)
Bali's largest and most modern shopping centre with boutiques selling international

brands as well as local designers, on the promenade. *Jl. Kartika Plaza | Tuban | www. discoveryshoppingmall.com*

EXTREME TOYS (U B4) *(₥ b4)*
Offbeat equipment and fashions for surfers, kite surfers and other fans of fun sports. *Kuta Square and Jl. Legian*

and you can take courses at the *Pro Surf School (Jl. Pantai Kuta* (U B4) *(₥ b4)* | *Kuta | tel. 0361 75 12 00 | www.prosurf school.com).* Those who want to go snorkelling or diving will have to drive a little further because the coast directly off Kuta is not suited for those activities. Tours and courses are organised by numerous firms

Surfers need not wait long for the perfect wave on Kuta's beaches

POKITO 1 (U B4) *(₥ b4)*
The top address for creative fashion for children, with modern batik motifs for little ones up to ten years of age. *Jl. Legian 384 | Kuta | www.koopukidz.com*

SCUBA DUBA DOO (U B4) *(₥ b4)*
The dive school's shop has absolutely everything you could need for diving and snorkelling. *Jl. Legian Kelod 367 | Legian*

SPORTS & ACTIVITIES

There are good surfing spots and places to hire equipment everywhere at the beach

including *Paradise Diving Indonesia (Jl. Arjuna 6a* (U A3) *(₥ a3)* | *Legian | tel. 0811 39 35 15 | www.b-a-l-i.com/english.htm).* There are beach massages and spas on every corner. The *DaLa Spa* in the *Villa de Daun Resort (Jl. Legian* (U B4) *(₥ b4)* | *Kuta | tel. 0361 8 50 10 22),* is considered to be one of Kuta's best but the treatments in *Cozy (Jl. Sunset Blok A3* (U B3) *(₥ b3)* | *Legian | tel. 0361 76 67 62)* are not quite as expensive. The *Waterbom Park (daily 9am–6pm | entrance fee US$31 | Jl. Kartika Plaza* (U B5) *(₥ b5)* | *Tuban | www.water bom-bali.com)* guarantees fun for the whole family.

ENTERTAINMENT

Kuta is the main nightlife area of Bali with countless clubs; the largest are on the *southern section of Jl. Legian*. The entertainment area around Jl. Arjuna, which used to be internationally famous, is moving more to Seminyak. A new entertainment centre is developing in so-called *New Kuta Beach* near Dreamland on the Bukit Peninsula.

BEACHWALK XXI PREMIERE ●
(U B4) (*b4*)

The luxurious cinema, that opened in 2012, mainly shows blockbusters from Hollywood and Asia. *Beachwalk Lantai 2, Jl. Pantai Kuta | Kuta | tel. 0361 8 46 56 21 | www.21cineplex.com/theaters*

EIKON (U B4) (*b4*)

Nightclub popular with Australians, there are theme evenings such as 'Mexican night' or 'bikini party'. *Daily 11pm–3am | Jl. Legian 178 | Kuta | tel. 0361 75 07 01*

M-BAR-GO (U B4) (*b4*)

Minimalist design and house music on the veranda; local DJs spin hip hop on the lower floor. *Daily 10pm–4am | Jl. Legian | Kuta | tel. 0361 75 62 80*

OCEAN'S 27 ☆
(U B5) (*b5*)

When the sun goes down this beach bar turns into a hip nightclub with international DJs at the turntables. *Daily 11am–4am | Discovery Esplanade | Jl. Kartika Plaza | Tuban | tel. 0361 75 60 27*

SKY GARDEN LOUNGE ☆
(U B4) (*b4*)

Celebrate with a spectacular view over the rooftops of Kuta: a mixed crowd spread over several dance floors and bars. ● Free cocktails served from 11pm to midnight. *Daily 7pm–4am | Jl. Legian 61 | Kuta | tel. 0361 75 63 62*

WHERE TO STAY

ALAM KUL KUL ☺
(U B4) (*b4*)

Boutique hotel that has won awards for its eco-friendly concept that unites traditional and modern elements; two restaurants and bar, two pools, spa and childcare – right on the beach. *79 rooms | Jl. Pantai Kuta | Legian | tel. 0361 75 25 19 | www.alamkulkul.com | Expensive*

DEKUTA BOUTIQUE HOTEL
(U B4) (*b4*)

Modern hotel catering to families, just steps away from the beach at Legian; with pool and two restaurants. *53 rooms | Jl. Pantai Kuta, Poppies Lane II | tel. 0361 75 38 80 | dekuta.com | Moderate*

O-CE-N BALI BY OUTRIGGER
(U B3) (*b3*)

Post-modern design hotel with two pools, spa, excellent beach restaurant and childcare facilities. *53 rooms | Jl. Arjuna 88 x | Legian Beach | tel. 0361 73 74 00 | www.outrigger.com | Expensive*

PADMA RESORT (U B3) (*b3*)

Large five-star beach hotel in modern Bali style with a variety of restaurants and bars, pool area and spa, sport and children's activities. *409 rooms | Jl. Padma 1 | Legian | tel. 0361 75 21 11 | www.padmaresortbali.com | Expensive*

POPPIES COTTAGES I (U B4) (*b4*)

A classic in Kuta: a narrow lane with small bungalows set in a tropical garden with pool; five minutes from the beach. *25 bungalows | Poppies Lane I | Kuta | tel. 0361 75 10 59 | www.poppiesbali.com | Moderate*

INSIDER TIP TANAYA BED & BREAKFAST
(U B3) (*b3*)

Reasonably-priced accommodation for budget travellers, with modern, clean rooms. Centrally located in Kuta. *7 rooms | Jl. Legian 131 | Kuta | tel. 0361 75 62 76 | www.tanayabed.com | Budget*

VILLA COCO (U B3) (*b3*)

The beach is ten minutes away from this secluded garden complex, with luxurious private villas, in the heart of Legian. Pool and in-house catering. *19 villas | Jl. Arjuna, Gang Villa Coco | Legian | tel. 0361 73 07 36 | www.villacoco.com | Expensive*

INFORMATION

KUTA TOURIST INFORMATION
(U B4) (*b4*)

Jl. Raya Kuta 2 | Kuta | tel. 0361 75 61 75

LOVINA

(130 C2) (*G1–2*) **Named after the English word 'love' by the last King of Buleleng, this 10km (6mi) coastline stretches to the west of Singaraja and includes the villages of Anturan, Kalibukbuk and Kaliasem.**

Inspired by the hippies and their peaceful invasion of Bali's north in the 1970s, the Prince realised his ideas of tourism here. Lovina lies on volcanic black sand beaches and the calm sea is ideal for swimming and snorkelling. Dolphin watching is the main attraction here. Every morning before sunrise, dozens of small outrigger boats set out for the reefs to show tourists the dolphins that can usually be found frolicking there. Lovinia has fewer guests than before and this has led to many of the hotels and sections of the beach becoming neglected and besieged by so-called guides looking for work. On the other hand, new resorts offering wellness, yoga and meditation holidays are being established at the foot of the nearby mountains. Lovina is an ideal starting point for excursions into the central highlands of Bali.

FOOD & DRINK

AKAR CAFE ☺

Small, fine and eco in every aspect: tasty vegetarian dishes, organic products, agency for yoga courses and even the décor is mint-green. *Jl. Binaria | Kalibukbuk | tel. 0819 15 62 55 25 | Budget–Moderate*

INSIDER TIP BAKERY LOVINA

This is the place for a healthy breakfast with muesli, whole-wheat bread and cheese, as well as a good wine selection and the best pizza in the north of Bali. *Jl. Raya Lovina | Kalibukbuk | tel. 0362 4 22 25 | Moderate*

MR. DOLPHIN

Popular, simple beach restaurant with good seafood. *Jl. Laviana | Banyualit | tel. 0813 53 27 69 85 | Budget*

SPORTS & ACTIVITIES

You can get diving and snorkelling equipment from your hotel or from *Spicedive (tel. 0362 4 15 09 | www.balispicedive.com)*, where you can also book tours and courses. Dolphin tours are offered everywhere on the beach and can also be organised by your accommodation. You will be able to learn massage techniques yourself in the *Araminth Spa (Jl. Mawar | Kalibukbuk | tel. 0812 3 81 25 04 | www.lifestylebali. com)*. Samyoga (Dusun Panti | tel. 0813 37 67 68 93 | www.samyogabali.com)* and the *Zen Resort Bali (Seririt | tel. 0362 9 35 78 | www.zenresortbali.com)* offer wellness and yoga holidays.

WHERE TO STAY

DAMAI LOVINA VILLAS ᢌ

Exquisite boutique hotel with 14 stylish bungalows, beautiful pool and spa. Near the mountains but with a view over the sea. Award-winning restaurant serving organic cuisine. *Jl. Damai | Kalibukbuk | tel. 0362 4 10 08 | www.damai.com | Expensive*

FRANGIPANI BEACH HOTEL

Chic boutique hotel right on the beach, with a view of the rice field. Pool and restaurant. *8 rooms | Jl. Kartika | Kalibukbuk | tel. 0812 3 82 47 79 | www.frangipani beachhotelbali.com | Moderate*

INSIDER TIP THE HAMSA RESORT ᢌ ☺

The 13 villas around a pool in a gigantic garden lie high up the mountain above the Singsing Waterfall with a view down to the sea. The services offered include an organic restaurant and Ayurvedic spa, yoga and detoxification treatments. *Jl. Air Terjun Sing Sing | Desa Cempaga | tel. 0812 46 16 89 12 | www.thehamsaresort.com | Moderate*

HOTEL MELAMUN

Simple, decent hotel with very good service and a beautiful swimming pool; three minutes from the beach. *10 rooms | Jl. Laviana 7 | Banyualit | tel. 0362 4 15 61 | www.hotelmelamun.com | Budget*

WHERE TO GO

BANJAR (130 B3) (*ⓜ F2*)

Famous for its hot springs *(Air Panas | daily 8am–6pm | entrance fee 5000 Rp)*, the village of Banjar is only 10km (6mi) to the west of Lovina. A short footpath leads to three pools with stone waterspouts. It is said that a dip in the 38°C

(100°F) sulphurous water has a curative effect. Bali's only Buddhist monastery the ● ᢌ *Brahmavihara Arama (daily 9am–6pm | entrance for a donation | brahmavi haraarama.com)* is south of Banjar. A garden with prayer halls climbs up the slope in several tiers: you can meditate there or simply enjoy the view down to the sea from high up. The monastery offers mediation stays lasting several days.

Treatments Indonesian style: bathing in the hot sulphur springs of Banjar

DANAU BRATAN ☀
(131 E3–4) (∅ H–J3)

The *Bratan Lake* stretches along the road from Singaraja to Bedugul around 20km (12mi) southeast of Lovina. Its main attraction is the fairytale 17th century *Pura Ulun Danu Bratan (daily 7am–7pm | entrance fee 30,000 Rp)*, one of the most important temples and a very popular photo opportunity. The eleven-tiered shrine, dedicated to the goddess of the lake, is located on a small island behind a beautiful garden. The Balinese take part in numerous ceremonies here to pray for sufficient water for their fields.

There are various accommodations and amusement parks near the lake: you can admire the 380 acres of *Botanical Gardens (daily 7am–6pm | Kebun Raya Eka Karya | entrance fee 7000 Rp, cars 12,000 Rp)* in *Candikuning* and also visit the *Bali Treetop Adventure Park (daily 8.30am–6pm | entrance fee US$21)*. There is an 18-hole golf course, hotel and spa the *Bali Handara Kosaido Country Club (www.bali handarakosaido.com)* north of the lake.

DANAU BUYAN AND TAMBLINGAN ★ ☀ (131 D3) (∅ H2)

The area around the Buyan and Tamblingan lakes, which once formed a single large crater lake, forms the fertile heart of Bali. A road passes coffee plantations on the high bank at the northern edge. You can walk to the village of *Munduk* (25km/16mi south of Lovina) on the southern shore, it is scenically located between mountain forests, orchards, and rice and tobacco fields. There is a 2km (1.2mi) path to a waterfall east of Munduk. If you stay at the ☀ ☺ INSIDER TIP *Puri Lumbung Cottages (tel. 0362 7 0128 87 | www.puri*

An idyll that can only be reached via narrow paths: Lake Tamblingan

umbung.com | *Moderate)*, an award-winning eco-resort with 23 cottages converted from old rice granaries with a view as far as the ocean, you will be able to relish the environment for even longer.

GITGIT WATERFALL
(131 D2) (*H2*)
About 17km (10mi) southeast of Lovina is Bali's highest waterfall which plummets around 40m (130ft) into the depths. A concrete path leads from the road to Bedugul past all kinds of kiosks and fruit trees to the natural pool *(daily 8am–5pm | entrance fee 10,000 Rp).*

SINGARAJA (131 D1) (*H1*)
With its population of 80,000, the old capital 10km (6mi) east of Lovina is the second largest town on the island. From here the Dutch established their control of Bali and the old harbour and many colonial buildings still bear witness to this period. Muslim and Chinese merchants had already settled here long before that and they still set the tone of life on the streets.
The old palace, the *Puri Agung (daily 9am–5pm | entrance for a donation | Jl. Mayor Metra 12 | tel. 0362 2 29 74)*, of the Kings of Buleleng was reconstructed at the beginning of the 20th century and today mainly exhibits pictures of the royal family whose descendants still live here. The *Museum Buleleng (Mon–Thu 7am–3pm, Fri 7am–11 am | entrance fee 5000 Rp | Jl. Veteran 23)* provides information on the history of the region and life of the last king. Next to it, you can visit the library founded by the Dutch in 1928, the *Gedong Kirtya (Mon–Thu 7am–3pm, Fri 7am–noon | entrance fee 10,000 Rp | Jl. Veteran 22)*, where more than 3000 old documents – including ornate lontar-leaf manuscripts and colonial writings – are preserved. There are several

impressive temples a few miles to the east of Singaraja. The erotic scenes and caricatures, which also include modern elements such as cars, in the *Pura Dalem* in *Sangsit* and *Jagaraga* show the more frivolous style of the north.

NUSA LEMBONGAN

(133 D1) (*L–M 6–7*) ★ Tourists who want to escape from all the hustle and bustle in the south of Bali will find what they are looking for here: the pace of life on the little island (4.5 × 2.5km/2.8 × 1.6mi) 12km (7.5mi) to the east off the coast of Sanur, is much slower and – with the exception of a few small vans – there are no cars.
Although there has been an increase in the number of resorts in the last ten years, most of the island's around 4000 inhabitants continue to live from seaweed cultivation. You will not find a post office or ATMs in the two villages of *Jungutbatu* and *Lembongan* (it is possible to exchange money at high rates) but there are seven small *temples* and an *underground house (daily | entrance fee 10,000 Rp).*
A long reef in the northwest has made Nusa Lembongan a popular destination for surfers. Snorkellers and divers can explore beautiful banks of coral around the neighbouring islands of *Nusa Ceningan* and *Nusa Penida*. The northeast is the region for trips through the mangroves while the secluded bays in the south will make you feel like a modern-day Robinson Crusoe. All of the accommodation is located on the western side of the island – many with spectacular views of the Gunung Agung.
The fastest way from Sanur to Nusa Lembongan is public ferry *(daily 8am,*

90 minutes/ 60,000 Rp, Perama | daily 10.3am, 90 minutes | 100,000 Rp | www. peramatour.com) or by speedboat *(30 minutes from US$25 | various providers | www.balitrips.net/lembongantransfers).* There are also speedboat connections with Padang Bai and the Gilis *(gili-fastboat.com).*

FOOD & DRINK

Most of the accommodations also run small cafés and there are simple *warungs* in the village. The hotel resorts in the southwest offer more elegant dining.

INSIDER TIP THE BEACH CLUB AT SANDY BAY
The small bay in the southeast of the island is the perfect place to chill out in the afternoon with a drink by the pool or to have a romantic dinner at night (collection service). *Sandy Bay | tel. 0828 97 00 56 56 | www.sandybaylembongan.com | Expensive*

BLUE CORNER BAR
The beach bar is part of the Blue Corner dive centre and eco resort and was built using natural materials. Its comfortable blue beanbag are ideal for sundowners – accompanied by tapas and beach volleyball. Instead of concrete walls, plants protect this stretch of the coastline from surf erosion. Waste recycling. *Blue Corner Beach | north of Jungutbatu | tel. 0819 16 23 10 54 | Budget*

SPORTS & ACTIVITIES

There are three popular spots for surfing right in front of *Jungutbatu* – they are popular with people on the beach too as there is always plenty to see. All of the accommodation options organise swimming and snorkelling trips to the more remote beaches. The possibilities for diving and snorkelling around *Nusa Ceningan* and *Nusa Penida* are excellent. Courses can be booked from *World Diving (Pondok Baruna | Jungutbatu | tel. 0812 3 90 06 86 | www.world-diving.com)* and Big Fish *(Secret Garden | Jungutbatu | tel. 0813 53 13 68 61 | www.bigfishdiving.com),* an organisation that supports initiatives to preserve the coral reefs. If you need to relax, *Yoga Shack (Secret Garden | Jungutbatu | tel. 0813 53 13 68 61 | www.yogashack lembongan.com)*, offers daily classes in its bamboo hut. The best way to explore the island is to hire a bicycle or moped from the place where you are staying.

BEACHES

Swimmers and surfers share the beach with seaweed farmers and fishermen in Jungutbatu. A steep path starting at *Coconut Beach* at the southern end of the main beach leads over the rocks to *Mushroom Bay,* which is also accessible by boat. From the village of Lembongan some bumpy roads lead to *Tamarind Bay,* secluded *Sandy Bay* and the wild and romantic **INSIDER TIP** *Dream Beach.*

WHERE TO STAY

INDIANA KENANGA
Luxurious boutique hotel with elegant pool and spa and excellent French cuisine. *8 suites | Jungutbatu | tel. 0366 55 93 71 | www.indiana-kenanga-villas. com | Expensive*

PONDOK BARUNA
One of the oldest hotels on the island with simple, clean rooms, pool and its own dive school. Good beach restaurant with friendly service. *22 rooms | Jungutbatu | tel. 0812 3 94 09 92 | www.world-diving. com | Budget*

WAKA NUSA RESORT ☆
Comfortable bungalow complex under coconut palms with pool, spa and restaurant, as well as a wide range of leisure activities. *10 bungalows | Mushroom Beach | tel. 0366 2 44 77 | www.waka experience.com | Expensive*

WHERE TO GO

NUSA PENIDA AND NUSA CENINGAN
(133 D–F 1–2) (*U L–N 6–8*)
Very few tourists stay on the larger of the neighbouring island of *Nusa Penida* but it is a popular destination for snorkelling and dive excursions. Once a prison island, the majority of the inhabitants are Muslims. However, most Balinese avoid the island because of the legend that this is the home of the evil giant Jero Gede Mecaling. Once or twice a year boats from Bali bring offerings on the temple anniversary of the *Pura Dalem Penataran Ped* in *Toyapakeh*, to appease the demon. At the time of the Galungan festival, there is a large procession to the *Goa Karangsari*, an enormous cave 10km (6mi) south of the main town *Sampalan*. The ☺ *Friends of the National Parks Foundation,* who are active in the protection of wild animals and their natural habitat, operate a *visitor centre (tel. 0828 97 60 86 96 | www.fnpf. org | Budget)* with a simple guesthouse for volunteer helpers in the middle of the bird sanctuary. Public ferries and charter boats depart from Nusa Lembongan for Toyapakeh.

Between Nusa Lembongan and Penida is the small island of *Nusa Ceningan* which can be reached on foot or by bicycle or moped over a narrow bridge from Nusa Lembongan. Recently a few small cafés and bungalows, including *Jenny's Bed & Breakfast (tel. 0812 36 27 76 50 | bsr_nuslem@yahoo.com | Budget)*, have opened their doors on the island.

PADANG BAI

(132 C6) (*U M5*) **For most tourists, the fishing village Bai (pop. 20,000) is merely a stopping-off place on their way to Lombok or the Gilis.**

Spectacular is the only word for the underwater world off Nusa Penida

The main bay is dominated by the ferry terminals but there are also guests who spend their entire holiday here. This is mainly due to the laid-back atmosphere and reasonably priced accommodation, as well as the outstanding dive sites: the coral reefs just off the coast and the islands of Nusa Penida and Nusa Ceningan in the south guarantee spectacular encounters with the colourful life underwater.

FOOD & DRINK

OZONE CAFE
A time-honoured institution that is popular with travellers and the locals alike. The cool drinks are accompanied by pizza and live music. *Jl. Segara | tel. 0363 4 15 01 | Budget*

TOPI INN CAFE
This cosy café serves breakfast with muesli, homemade cakes and a Balinese buffet and seafood in the evening. Reading and games corner. *Jl. Silayukti 99 | tel. 0363 4 14 24 | www.topiinn.nl | Budget*

SPORTS & ACTIVITIES

Padang Bai is one of Bali's most important starting points for dive tours. There are numerous enterprises on the main beach offering courses; the diving school *Paradise Diving Indonesia (Jl. Silayukti 9 Bi | tel. 0361 7 42 85 01 | www.b-a-l-i.com/english.htm)* and *Water Worx (Jl. Silayukti | tel. 0363 4 12 20 | www.waterworxbali.com)* are recommended. Fishing tours in a traditional boat are the speciality of *Pak Lulu (tel. 0813 37 76 80 77)*.

BEACHES

You will be more tempted to just watch the ferries and diving boats at the main beach in Padang Bai than to go for a swim there, two nice swimming and snorkelling beaches are *Blue Lagoon Beach* on the other side of the hill to the east of the main beach, as well as the 'small beach' *Bias Tugal,* which is usually called *White Sand Beach* and is a 15-minute walk along a footpath along the hill west of the ferry

port (be careful: the currents here are very strong!).

WHERE TO STAY

BLOO LAGOON VILLAGE ⚛ ☺
Eco-resort catering to families, right above Blue Lagoon Beach; spacious villas, pool, spa and organic restaurant. *24 villas | tel. 0363 4 12 11 | www.bloolagoon.com | Expensive*

INSIDER TIP▶ LEMON HOUSE ⚛
Spotlessly clean hotel for budget travellers taht can be reached via some steep steps from the harbour; the terrace has a splendid view over the entire bay. *3 rooms, 4 dormitory beds | Gang Melanting 5 | tel. 0812 39 89 67 50 | www.lemonhouse.me | Budget*

HOTEL PURI RAI
The two-storey complex, with three pools and a popular restaurant, is the most comfortable place to stay in the village. *30 rooms | Jl. Silayukti 7 | tel. 0363 4 13 85 | www.purirai hotels.com | Budget–Moderate*

WHERE TO GO

GOA LAWAH (132 C6) *(𝜙 M5)*
The 'Bat Cave' with one of the six most sacred temples on Bali is only 5km (3mi) west of Padang Bai. At dusk, the bats leave the cave with a deafening noise. The cave – like the temple – is covered with a thick coating of their excrement. *Daily 8am–6pm | entrance fee 10,000 Rp.*

KLUNGKUNG (SEMARAPURA)
(132 B6) *(𝜙 L5)*
This market town (16km/10mi) with a population of 50,000 was once the main residence of the first Hindu kings of Bali. When the successor to the throne of the powerful Majapahit Empire was forced to

View from the Kerta Gosa to Bale Kembang in Klungkung

flee in 15th century from the Muslim conquerors of Java, he settled in Gelgel near Klungkung and proclaimed himself ruler of Bali. In 1710, the Gelgel dynasty moved their seat to Klungkung. The only remains of the former glory are a palace gate, the old court hall Kerta Gosa and the Bale Kembang ('floating pavilion'), which can be visited today in the Taman Gili (daily 8am–5pm | entrance fee 5000 Rp). The Kerta Gosa in particular, with its elaborate wayang style ceiling paintings, is very impressive: judgement was pronounced here, beneath depictions of heavenly pleasures and hellish punishments, until 1950. The larger Bale Kembang most recently served as the court's waiting room. The frescoes depict scenes from myths and legends, as well as Balinese everyday life in times gone by. The rest of the palace was destroyed during the Dutch conquest in 1908. The Puputan Monument in front of the complex commemorates the entire courts

ritual suicide to avoid colonisation. The Semarajaya Museum – which documents the history, as well as everyday life to the present day – is also part of the Taman Gili.

In 2010, the artist Nyoman Gunarsa opened the museum named after him (daily 9am–4pm | entrance fee 25,000 Rp | Jl. Petigaan Banda 1 | Takmung), which is one of the largest art museums on Bali, 3km (2mi) to the west of Klungkung. His studio is also within the museum.

PEMUTERAN

(128 C2) (*∅ C2*) **The fishing village at the north-western tip of Bali, on the edge of the West Bali National Park, has developed into an exclusive destination for snorkellers, divers and nature lovers.** Most of the establishments on the peaceful beaches are upscale resorts with full

Divers discover some bizarre under-water worlds off Bali's northwest coast

hand in hand on the project which has proven very successful. The *Reef Seen Aquatics (tel. 0362 9 30 01 | www.reefseen. com)* diving centre also operates a turtle station.

FOOD & DRINK

INSIDER TIP CAFÉ BALI BALANCE ☺

On offer are homemade whole-wheat bread and delicious cakes, fresh fruit juices and salads – and the profits go to a local school project. *Jl. Raya Singaraja-Gilimanuk | Banyupoh | tel. 0853 37 45 54 54 | www.bali-balance.com | Budget*

WHERE TO STAY

MATAHARI BEACH RESORT ☺

Luxury hotel complex in a fabulous location on the beach, with an award-winning restaurant, excellent spa, pool and numerous leisure activities. The hotel supports a number of social projects that aid the children in the village. *32 rooms | tel. 0362 9 23 12 | www.matahari-beach-resort.com | Expensive*

INSIDER TIP THE MENJANGAN ☺

This eco-resort with a pool, spa and panoramic restaurant – all built using natural materials and designed to fit into the surroundings – has an idyllic location between mangroves and the jungle. Excellent variety of tours. *23 bungalows | Jl. Raya Gilimanuk-Singaraja 17km | Desa Pejarakan | tel. 0362 9 47 00 | www. themenjangan.com | Expensive*

service: almost every hotel has a restaurant, a spa, its own dive school and organises tours to the national park. There are some less expensive homestays in the village itself. The world's largest project for establishing artificial coral reefs is off the coast of Pemuteran. The village inhabitants, the hotel owners and scientists work

PONDOK SARI BEACH RESORT ☺

The 35 bungalows with open-air baths – the water is processed in an environmentally friendly way – restaurant, pool and dive school are scattered through a beautiful garden with lotus ponds. *tel. 0362 9 23 37 | www.pondoksari.com | Moderate*

SUKASARI HOMESTAY

Family-run bungalow complex, three minutes from the beach, authentic restaurant and lovely garden. *6 rooms | tel. 0813 38 26 28 29 | sukasarihomestay. com | Budget*

WHERE TO GO

PULAU MENJANGAN ⭐
(128 B1) *(∅ B1)*

The uninhabited island off the northwest tip of the national park is considered Bali's best dive area, with an exceptional diversity of coral and fish. Experts will be delighted at the precipitous reefs and a shipwreck while the coral protection project near the beach guarantees enjoyment for beginners and snorkellers. The island is also the site of what is said to be Bali's oldest temple (still preserved in its original state) the *Pura Gili Kencana*; it was supposedly built in the 14th century at a time when the Javanese Majapahit Empire still controlled large sections of what is now Indonesia.

BOOKS & FILMS

▶ **Earth Dance** – In her novel, Oka Rusmini tells the tale of three generations of women who love, live and suffer under the caste system in Bali (2007)

▶ **Art and Culture of Bali** – Standard work on culture and religion on Bali by the ethnologist Urs Ramseyer (2002)

▶ **Love and Death in Bali** – Vicki Baum's classic novel (2007) describes the dramatic events that led to the ritual suicide of the royal court of Bandung in 1906

▶ **A Short History of Bali** – Interesting overview of the entire history of Bali by Robert Pringle (2004) a diplomat with a degree in Southeast Asian history

▶ **Bali – 1000 Faces of an Island** – Travel documentary directed by Andreas Zerr (USA 2006) that journeys through the island visiting its stunning dive and surf locations, its picturesque villages and temples

▶ **Eat, Pray, Love** – Parts of the Hollywood film based on the best-seller by Elizabeth Gilbert, and starring Julia Roberts, were filmed on Bali in 2009

▶ **The Year of Living Dangerously** – The film (1982) adaptation of the novel by Christopher Koch takes place in Indonesia during the political turmoil of a coup to overthrow President Sukarno. Mel Gibson plays the role of a young reporter and his love interest is played by Sigourney Weaver

▶ **A House in Bali** – This entertaining memoir by composer Colin McPhee (first published in 1947) is the story of his time in Bali documenting gamelan music and all aspects of life on the island in the colonial era

▶ **Sacred & Secret** – The Swiss filmmaker Basil Gelpke documents the religious and social life on Bali through the eyes of Prince Tjokorda Raka Kerthyasa (2010)

PURA AGUNG PULAKI
(129 D2) (*C2*)

The temple on the coast was rebuilt in 1983 against a dramatic backdrop of cliffs and jungle and commemorates the arrival of the Javanese Hindu priest Nirartha on Bali in the 16th century. The Pura Agung Pulaki is surrounded by three additional temples and is now notorious for the hordes of monkeys that live there as guards. *Daily 8am–6pm | entrance for a donation*

TAMAN NASIONAL BALI BARAT
(128–129 A–F 2–5) (*A–F 2–4*)

West Bali National Park covers an area of over 47,000 acres from the coral reefs in the northwest, the mangroves and arid stretches, to mountain forests on the slopes of volcanoes. 160 different bird species – some of them, very rare – live here in addition to various kinds of monkeys, wild buffaloes, dwarf deer, monitor lizards and snakes. It is possible to drive through the park on your own initiative if you stay on the main road or if you just want to go snorkelling at the beach. However, you have to make use of the services of a registered guide for jeep, boat and trekking tours *(entrance fee 25,000 Rp)*. Most of the treks start from the visitor centre in *Labuhan Lalang,* which is also the point of departure for boats to Pulau Menjangan.

SANUR

(135 D4) (*J–K 6–7*) **Sanur (pop. 35,000) is Kuta's more tranquil counterpart and is ideal for a family holiday.**
The sea is calm and so shallow that children can splash around in it; however, it is only possible to swim at high tide. There is a paved path lined with beach bars and cafés all the way along the seaside with the lush gardens of the hotel complexes with their pools behind it. The only high-rise building on Bali was built in the north; today it houses the Inna Grand Bali Beach Hotel. After its construction the government forbade any further high-rise buildings. There are many lovely shops and good restaurants on long *Jl. Danau Tamblingan*. The spectacular *Kite Festival* in the north of Sanur attracts a great number of visitors every year in July/August, as does the *Sanur Village Festival* with art markets, traditional performances, music and water sports activities, which also takes place in July and August.

SIGHTSEEING

MUSEUM LE MAYEUR
The Belgian artist Adrien-Jean Le Mayeur – 'Indonesia's Gauguin'– lived in Bali from 1932 until shortly before his death in 1958. The museum in the house he once lived displays his work, with many portraits of his wife Ni Pollock, a famous dancer. The museum shop sells art and handicrafts *Mon–Thu 8am–3.30pm, Fri/Sat 8am–1pm | entrance fee 20,000 Rp | on the beach path near Jl. Hang Tuah | tel. 0361 28 62 01*

FOOD & DRINK

CAFE BATU JIMBAR ☺
Fresh juices, homemade cakes and vegetarian dishes are served in a simple, design atmosphere; organic market on Sunday. *Jl. Danau Tamblingan 75A | tel. 0361 28 73 74 | Moderate*

INSIDER TIP GREENLEAF WARUNG ORGANIC ☺
A cosy little restaurant that specialises in Indonesian cuisine served with organic rice and vegetables. *Jl. Tandakan 7 | Sindhu | tel. 0361 3 18 71 00 | Budget*

RISTORANTE MASSIMO
Classic Italian restaurant that is a perennial favourite: very good pizza, *antipasti* and *gelati*; perfect service. *Jl. Danau Tamblingan 206 | tel. 0361 28 89 42 | Moderate*

PREGINA
Simple, but tastefully decorated, restaurant serving excellent Balinese dishes at reasonable prices. *Jl. Danau Tamblingan 106 | tel. 0361 7 66 23 97 | Budget*

SHOPPING

The entire path along the seaside is lined with souvenir shops.

GUDANG KERAMIK
The outlet of *Jenggala Keramik* offers attractive, inexpensively priced, ceramic ware. *Jl. Danau Tamblingan 97 | www.jenggala-bali.com*

MANIK ORGANIK ☺
This is the place to stock up on organic food, natural cosmetics and bags made from recycled materials, as well as yoga and meditation accessories. Environmental organisations also hold breakfast meetings here. *Jl. Danau Tamblingan 85 | www.manikorganikbali.com*

NOGO BALI
Clothes, decorations and accessories made from hand-woven cotton fabric as well as antique *ikat*, which can also be made according to the client's wishes. *Jl. Danau Tamblingan 98 | www.nogobali.com*

SUARTI MAESTRO
The designer Suarti describes her jewellery based on old Indonesian models as 'wearable art'. *Jl. Bypass Ngurah Rai 104 | www.suartimaestro.com*

SPORTS & ACTIVITIES

Most places offering accommodation also arrange fishing and snorkelling tours in the south of Bali. The surfing spots near Sanur are not as spectacular as those on the west side of the island. *Crystal Divers*

Holiday idyll: hotels in the midst of tropical gardens in Sanur

One of the inhabitants of the Bali Safari & Marine Park

(Jl. Danau Tamblingan 168 | tel. 0361 28 67 37 | www.crystal-divers.com) organises good dive courses. The majority of the large hotels have tennis courts, the *Inna Grand Bali Beach Hotel (Jl. Hang Tuah Sanur | www.innagrandbalibeach.com)* even has a nine-hole golf course. The ☺ *Jamu Traditional Spa* in the Tandjung Sari Hotel *(Jl. Danau Tamblingan 41 | tel. 0361 28 65 95 | www.jamutraditionalspa. com)* offers relaxing treatments using natural local products.

ENTERTAINMENT

There are chic cocktail bars in the large hotels and many beach cafés offer live music.

ARENA PUB & BAR

This restaurant-bar has billiards and live sports broadcasts, a quiz on Wednesday night and live music and a billiards tournament on Friday, and is very popular with many foreigners living on Bali. *Daily noon–1am | Bypass Ngurah Rai 115 | tel. 0361 28 72 55*

CAT & FIDDLE

Pub run by the British Honorary Consul on Bali that offers Guinness and live Irish music. *Daily to midnight | Jl. Cemara 36 | tel. 0361 28 22 18*

INSIDER TIP ▶ PIANO BAR

Romantic cocktail bar located on a lotus pond in the lush garden of the Grand Hyatt Hotel; daily live music, from jazz to R & B. *Daily 10am–1am | Jl. Danau Tamblingan 89 | tel. 0361 28 12 34*

WHERE TO STAY

INSIDER TIP ▶ FLASHBACKS

Small, tasteful complex with lovely bungalows and one suite; mini pool and café; five minutes from the beach. *9 rooms | Jl. Danau Tamblingan 106 | tel. 0361 28 16 82 | www.flashbacks-chb.com | Budget– Moderate*

HOTEL JATI & HOMESTAY
Eleven simple rooms in Balinese style and a villa for longer stays. Pool and beautiful garden, relaxed atmosphere. *Jl. Danau Tamblingan 168–170 | tel. 0361 28 17 30 | www.hoteljatiandhomestay.com | Budget*

PURI SANTRIAN
Comfortable hotel complex with private beach and beach club, pool, spa and excellent restaurant. *182 rooms | Jl. Pantai Sanur | tel. 0361 28 80 09 | www.santrian. com/puri | Moderate–Expensive*

RESPATI BEACH HOTEL
Small, modern hotel complex with two pools and restaurant bar right on the beach. *35 rooms | Jl. Danau Tamblingan 33 | tel. 0361 28 84 27 | www.raspatibeach hotel.com | Moderate*

TANDJUNG SARI
The nostalgic bungalow complex with its ornate décor was one of Bali's first beach-front hotels in the 1960s. Pool, spa, restaurant and reading lounge. *26 Bungalows | Jl. Danau Tamblingan 41 | tel. 0361 28 84 41 | www.tandjungsarihotel.com | Expensive*

THE ZEN VILLAS
Five comfortably furnished holiday villas with their own kitchen and private pool in the centre of Sanur. *Jl. Kesari 2 No. 3 B | Sanur | tel. 0361 28 61 29 | www.thezen villas.com | Expensive*

WHERE TO GO

BALI SAFARI & MARINE PARK
(135 E3) *(ᗰ K6)*
The popular safari park 23km (14mi) northeast of Sanur is home to more than 50 species of animals – some of them endangered – including white tigers, Komodo dragons, and Sumatra elephants (elephant rides also available). The visitors travel through the open zoo, which conforms to international standards, by truck. Award-winning restaurant and hotel. *Daily 9am–5pm | entrance fee US$49 | Jl. Bypass. Dr. Ida Bagus Mantra 19.8km | Gianyar | www.balisafarimarinepark.com*

BENOA (134–135 C–D5) *(ᗰ J7)*
Established by the Dutch, Bali's most important port, Labuhan Benoais, is located south of Sanur. Ships with freight for nearby Denpasar anchor here as do the Pelni passenger ships that call at all parts of Indonesia. This is also the departure point for the speedboats to Nusa Lembongan and the Gilis.

PULAU SERANGAN
(135 D5) *(ᗰ J7)*
The island owes its name to the sea turtles that used to come here in great numbers to lay their eggs. Today, you will need a great deal of luck to see one of these endangered animals outside of the turtle station that was established in 2006 – in spite of a ban, they are still being hunted. The south of the small 180 acre island is lined with secluded beaches shaded by palm trees and there is a rather inconspicuous temple, the *Pura Sakenan*, in the north. It is the site of processions held at important ceremonies intended to appease the gods of the sea. A bridge connects the island with the belt of mangroves to the south of Sanur; boat trips are operated from *Tanjung Benoa*.

SEMINYAK

(134 C4) *(ᗰ H7)* ★ At a time when Kuta was still a village and Denpasar a long way away, the rich and famous built their villas in the rice fields around the village of Seminyak.

Today, the town (official pop. 4000) joins seamlessly with Denpasar's Kerobokan suburb in the north, while the former promenade *Jl. Arjuna* forms the boundary to Legian. Restaurants and boutiques line the former beach road to the Hotel Oberoi, *Jl. Laksmana*. However, Seminyak is completely different from Kuta and Legian – here, things are little more chic, exclusive and expensive. The beach and waves are just as beautiful as in Kuta – but not so crowded – and the beach bars reflect the latest design trends. The construction boom has now also extended to the neighbouring villages of *Petitenget*, *Batubelig* and *Canggu*, the surfers' paradise. But, there are still some resorts amidst the rice fields and the beach is empty enough that one can ride along the drift line on horseback.

FOOD & DRINK

BALE BALI
Good Chinese and Indonesian cuisine; jazz in the evening. *Jl. Kunti 4 BB | Seminyak | tel. 0361 73 27 31 | Budget–Moderate*

INSIDER TIP BIKU ☺
The antique furnishing and cake buffet in the bookshop's teahouse promise a pleasant afternoon. Many dishes are prepared using organic ingredients. *Jl. Raya Petitenget 88 | Kerobokan | tel. 0361 8 57 08 88 | www.bikubali.com | Moderate*

ECHO BEACH HOUSE
Tasty treats in a *warung* setting right on the beach; DJs in the evening and live music on Sundays. *Echo Beach | Canggu | tel. 0361 7 47 46 04 | Moderate*

LA LUCCIOLA ☼
The airy, two-storey beach restaurant serves brunch and fine Italian cuisine. *Jl.*

Pura Telaga Waja | Petitenget | tel. 0361 73 08 38 | Expensive

MAMASAN
Restaurant and lounge in 1920s Shanghai style, with excellent Asian set meals prepared by the celebrated chef Will Meyrick. *Jl. Raya Kerobokan 135 | Kerobokan | tel. 0361 73 94 36 | www.mamasanbali.com | Expensive*

SHOPPING

DOWN TO EARTH ☺
Organic, vegetarian supermarket with an attached café and restaurant, they also have a delivery service. *Jl. Laksmana 99 | Seminyak | www.downtoearthbali.com*

JEMME
Glamorous jewellery by the British designer Luke Stockley; some inspired by Balinese motifs. Exquisite fusion cuisine in the affiliated restaurant. *Jl. Raya Petitenget 28 | Kerobokan | www.jemmebali.com*

LUCY'S BATIK
Creative fashion and furnishing accessories using handmade cotton batik fabrics; ideal as souvenirs. *Jl. Raya Basangkasa 88 | Seminyak and J. Dewi Sri 88 | Legian | www.lucysbatik.com*

NILUH DJELANTIK
Well-known Balinese shoe designer who counts Cameron Diaz and Gisele Bündchen among her clients. *Jl. Raya Kerobokan 144 | Kerobokan | niluhdjelantik.tumblr.com*

SIMPLEKONSEPSTORE ☺
Fashion, household goods and all kinds of objects in a melange of Italian designs and traditional styles; supports Eco Bali Recycling. *Jl. Laksmana 40 | Seminyak | tel. 0361 73 03 93 | www.sksbali.com*

Every evening, holidaymakers enjoy lavish cocktails in the Ku Dé Ta

SPORTS & ACTIVITIES

As is the case in Kuta, almost everything in Seminyak revolves around the beach and surfing. Surf courses can be booked from *Rip Curl (Jl. Arjuna | Legian/Seminyak | tel. 0361 73 58 58 | www.ripcurlschool ofsurf.com).*

There are also numerous spa services, pamper yourself with a day in the energy-efficient 😊 INSIDER TIP *Private Spa Wellness Center (Jl. Camplung Tanduk 4 | Seminyak | tel. 0361 73 16 48 | www.privatespawellnesscenter.com)* with a great variety of Far Eastern therapies, natural products and thermal treatments. The impressive ● *Prana Spa (Jl. Kunti 118 X | Seminyak | tel. 0361 73 08 40 | www.the villas.net)* provides exquisite treatments in a décor straight out of the Arabian Nights: Ayurvedic therapies, Balinese herbal scrubs, reflexology and Turkish steam baths. A little less expensive is the Mediterranean atmosphere of *Bodyworks (Jl. Kayu Jati 2 | Petitenget | tel. 0361 73 33 17 | www.bodyworksbali.com)* with a wide selection of massage and body care therapies.

There are wonderful horseback rides along the beach and through the rice fields in Canggu with *Horse Adventure Bali (Pereran | Canggu | tel. 0361 3 65 55 97 | www.balihorseadventure.com).*

ENTERTAINMENT

HU'U

Chic restaurant bar in a romantic setting with a pool, international bands and DJs. Sun–Thu 11.30am–1am, Fri/Sat 11.30am–3am | Jl. Laksmana | Petitenget | tel. 0361 73 64 43

KU DÉ TA ⚜

Design lounge on the beach of the Oberoi Hotel; Australian fusion cuisine, cocktail bar, cool guests. *Daily to 1am | Jl. Laksmana 9 | Seminyak | tel. 0361 73 69 69*

POTATO HEAD 🍴
Chic, multi-level beach club in unusual design with gigantic pool bar and two acclaimed restaurants, international bands. *Daily 11am–2am | Jl. Petitenget | Seminyak | tel. 0361 4 73 79 79*

SOS SUPPER CLUB 🍴
The rooftop bar of the Anantara Resort serves wonderful cocktails and tapas as the sun sets and afterwards international DJs spin lounge music. *Sun–Tue 4pm–11pm, Wed–Sat 4pm–1am | Jl. Abimanyu | Seminyak | tel. 0361 73 77 73*

WHERE TO STAY

INSIDER TIP▶ VILLA BLUBAMBU
Chic homestay with two pools and spa service in a beautiful garden; five minutes from the beach. *3 villas | Jl. Abimanyu | Gang Melon | Seminyak | tel. 0818 05 59 30 85 | www.villablubambu.com | Moderate*

DESA SENI ☺
Guests in this eco-resort will feel like they are living in a village surrounded by rice fields. The resort offers tastefully furnished, antique wooden bungalows, pool, spa and organic restaurant. Also art and yoga courses; ten minutes from the beach. *10 bungalows | Jl. Subak Sari 13 | Pantai Berawa | Canggu | tel. 0361 8 44 63 92 | www.desaseni.com | Expensive*

LEGONG KERATON BEACH HOTEL
A little way outside of Canggu, this unassuming, modern beach hotel has a good restaurant, pool and spa and is set in a lovely garden right on the beach. Friendly service. *40 rooms | Pantai Berawa | Canggu | tel. 0361 4 73 02 80 | www.legongkeratonhotel.com | Moderate*

TEKA-TEKI HOUSE
Clean, quiet and very friendly homestay in the heart of Seminyak. *5 rooms | Jl. Drupadi 1 | Gg Puri Kubu 23 | Seminyak | tel. 0361 8 47 58 12 | Budget*

TONY'S VILLAS
Secluded bungalow complex in modern Bali style, restaurant and pool with bar, two minutes from the beach. *22 rooms, 9 villas | Jl. Petitenget | Kerobokan | tel. 0361 4 73 61 66 | www.balitonys.com | Expensive*

WHERE TO GO

BALI BIRD PARK (135 D3) (𝄞 J6)
250 different species of exotic birds flutter around in Bali's bird park around 25km (16mi) northeast of Seminyak. A jungle-like reptile park with snakes, lizards and Komodo dragons is integrated into it. *Daily 9am–5.30pm | entrance fee US$23.50 | Jl. Serma Cok Ngurah Gambir Singapadu | Batubulan*

GUNUNG BATUKARU ★
(130–131 C–D4) (𝄞 G–H 3–4)
Bali's second highest volcano (2276m/7467ft) is considered the island's 'rice basket'. When the weather is clear, you can see as far as the ocean from the spectacular *Jatiluwih rice terraces* on the south side. The *Pura Luhur Batukaru (daily 7am–6pm | entrance for a donation),* one of the six holiest temples, lies to the west at an altitude of 825m (2707ft) about 50km (31mi) from Seminyak. The origins of the enchanted complex, hidden in the forest, date back to the 11th century. It is said a Hindu priest from Java founded the temple here to honour the spirits of the Bratan, Buyan and Tamblingan lakes. A seven-tiered shrine is dedicated to the mountain god Maha Dewa. Today, the complex functions as the ancestral temple of the court of Tabanan. Those who

want to explore the mountain in more detail can spend the night in the 😊 INSIDER TIP *Sarinbuana Eco Lodge (4 bungalows | tel. 0361 7435198 | baliecolodge.com | Expensive).*

MENGWI (134 C2) (𝄞 J5)
In 1634, the King of Mengwi had the *Pura Taman Ayun* built as the family sanctuary and it is today still the second largest temple complex in Bali. It is around 25km (16mi) north of Seminyak in a beautiful, spacious garden surrounded by a moat full of lotus flowers. The water temple is the centrepiece of the sophisticated *subak* system that irrigates the rice fields in Bali. The traditional system is both democratic and ecologically sustainable. A bridge leads to the split entrance gate of the temple. The innermost of the three courtyards can only be entered when important ceremonies are being held but it is possible to get a glimpse of the holy shrines by looking over the outer wall. *Daily 8am–5pm | entrance fee 15,000 Rp.*

NEGARA (128 C4–5) (𝄞 C3–4)
The capital city of Jembrana (pop. 40,000, around 100km/62mi west of Seminyak), is the most sparsely populated region on Bali, and is mainly known for the buffalo races *(mekepung)* that are held there during the dry season. The region has little in the way of tourist infrastructure, except at the beach at *Medewi,* which is a good surf spot.

PURA TANAH LOT (134 B3) (𝄞 H6)
Hundred of cameras can be heard clicking when the sun sinks behind the picturesque seaside temple Tanah Lot (15km/9mi northwest). This is Bali's most popular tourist scene. As can be expected, there are also countless hawkers and guides along the path from the car park to the rock where the temple is located and

At low tide, you can reach the Pura Tanah Lot without even getting your feet wet

visitors will have to run the gauntlet to get there. However, if you come to the sacred spot in the early morning, you will really be able to enjoy it. In a cavern beneath the rock, sea snakes, which are revered as sacred, guard the temple against evil. *Daily 7am–8pm | entrance fee 15,000 Rp.*

TABANAN (134 B2) (*ω H5*)

The small town 35km (22mi) northwest of Seminyak is home to Bali's *Subak Museum (daily 8am–5pm | entrance fee 5000 Rp)*, which provides fascinating insights into the cultivation and irrigation of the rice fields. Around 6km (4mi) north of Tabanan there is also a *Butterfly Park (daily 9am–5pm | entrance fee 80,000 Rp)*, where hundreds of exotic butterflies flutter about.

UBUD

(135 D2) (*ω J–K5*) ⭐ **The cultural and spiritual centre of Bali (pop. 70,000) lies between lush rice terraces and dramatic gorges. As early as the 8th century the Campuan area was declared a holy place by Buddhist monks.**

A branch of the Sukawati dynasty settled in Ubud in the 19th century and built a palace here. In the 1930s Prince Cokorda Gede Agung Sukawati, together with the German Walter Spies and Dutchman Rudolf Bonnet, founded the famous Pita Maha School of Painting here and the movement later paved the way for Western artists and intellectuals thereby helping the local art scene to achieve the extraordinary importance it has to this day.

Spiritual tourism is a somewhat more recent development: yoga and meditation courses are offered on almost every corner and organic food and drink are now a matter of course. Once a year, at the time of the INSIDER TIP *Bali Spirit Festival (www.balispiritfestival.com)*, Ubud is transformed into an international yoga camp with lots of dancing and music.

Today, the neighbouring villages from *Campuan* to *Tebesaya* have long become integrated into Ubud. There is an almost endless row of shops, restaurants and hotels along long *Monkey Forest Road*

WHERE TO START?
Junction in front of Ubud Palace: this is the heart of Ubud and also the site of the market and central tourist office. Monkey Forest Road leads south past countless boutiques and cafés until it reaches the Monkey Forest itself. Take Jl. Ubud Raya to the west and after about 100 yards you will reach the Puri Lukisan, the Blanco Museum (a further 800m/2625ft) and the Neka Museum after just over half a mile further.

and, in spite of being so narrow, the traffic creates the feeling of a being in a large city. However, not far away, people out for a walk will come across lush rice fields, rushing rivers and forests to gladden any nature lover's heart.

SIGHTSEEING

AGUNG RAI MUSEUM OF ART (ARMA)

This museum in a lovely park exhibits works by Balinese artists, Spies, Bonnet, Le Mayeur and the famous Javanese painter Affandi. Charming café ● and various courses for tourists. *Daily 9am–6pm | entrance fee 40,000 Rp | Jl. Pengosekan | www.armabali.com*

THE BLANCO MUSEUM

The eccentric paintings of the Spanish-Philippine artist Antonio Blanco, who died in 1999, can be admired in this palace-like private residence. As in Blanco's art, the building's architecture and furnishings combine European and Balinese elements. *Daily 9am–5pm | entrance fee 50,000 Rp | Jl. Raya Campuan (directly behind the bridge) | www.blancomuseum.com*

GALLERIES ●

The *Komaneka Gallery (Monkey Forest Road | gallery.komaneka.com)* and the *Tony Raka Art Gallery (Jl. Raya Mas | www.tonyrakaartgallery.com)* are focused on modern artists from Bali and Java. The *Seniwati Gallery (Jl. Sriwedari 2 B | www.seniwatigallery.com)*, on the other hand, promotes female Balinese artists. Contemporary Indonesian and international art is displayed – and can be bought – in *Gaya Fusion (Jl. Raya Sayan | www.gayafusion.com)* and *Sika Gallery (Jl. Raya Campuan | www.sikagallery.com)*.

MONKEY FOREST

Around 300 long-tailed monkeys live in a sacred forest, where they cheekily demand peanuts and other food from the visitors. There are three temples here: a small bathing temple and a cremation temple *(Pura Prajapati)*, as well as the larger *Pura Dalem Agung*, which is guarded by seven figures of witches. A giant stone turtle, with snakes entwined around its body, rests in the door to the inner courtyard. *Daily 8am–6pm | entrance fee 20,000 Rp | www.monkeyforestubud.com*

NEKA ART MUSEUM

The collection of the art patron Suteja Neka provides an excellent overview of modern Balinese art from the 20th century to the present day, as well as works by the Dutchmen Rudolf Bonnet and Arie Smit. *Daily 9am–5pm | entrance fee 50,000 Rp | Jl. Raya Sanggingan | Campuan | www.museumneka.com*

PURI LUKISAN

A bridge leads into the lush green park of this 'Painting Palace' that was opened in 1953. Works in the old *wayang* style, as well as by young artists and the Pita Maha school of Rudolf Bonnet and Walter Spies, are displayed in several buildings. In addition, there are works by contemporary Balinese artists and the famous I Gusti Nyoman Lempad. *Daily 9am–5pm | entrance fee 50,000 Rp | Jl. Raya Ubud | www.mpl-ubud.com*

Contemporary Balinese art on display in the Neka Art Museum

PURI SAREN (UBUD PALACE)

Ubud Palace, which is still the home of the descendants of the last king, is located at the central junction in the town. There are several beautifully decorated buildings from the 19th century in the well maintained garden and dance performances are held in the main courtyard in the evening. *Daily 8am–6pm, performance daily 7.30pm | free admission, dance 80,000 Rp*

An abundance of exotic fruits in Ubud's markets

FOOD & DRINK

ALCHEMY 😊
Raw food – not only for vegans. Large selection of salads, juices and desserts. *Jl. Penestanan Kelod (turn off behind the Blanco Museum) | tel. 0361 971981 | Moderate*

IBU OKA
Unassuming *warung* where Bali's most famous *babi guling* (sucking pig) is served. *Jl. Tegal Sari 2 (opposite Ubud Palace) | tel. 0361 976345 | Budget*

KAFE@BALISPIRIT 😊
Organic café with an extensive breakfast menu, delicious cakes and salads, as well as yoga courses. Novel furnishing and fittings made using recycled materials. *Jl. Hanoman 44 B | tel. 0361 7803802 | Moderate*

MELTING WOK WARUNG
A French Laotian couple treats diners to delicious Southeast Asian meals at reasonable prices. *Jl. Gootama 13 | tel. 0821 53 66 60 87 | Moderate*

MOZAIC
One of Bali's best restaurants: chef Chris Salans previously worked in New York and creates remarkable multi-course set meals every evening. *Jl. Raya Sanggingan | Campuan | tel. 0361 97 5768 | Expensive*

INSIDER TIP ⯈ SARI ORGANIK BODAG MALIAH ⚲ 😊
Freshly-pressed juice and crispy salads are served amidst the rice fields of the Sari Organik permaculture farm. Twenty minutes walk from the centre of town; pick-up service. *Subak Sok Wayah | tel. 0361 972087 | Moderate*

TUT MAK
Popular restaurant with Mediterranean cooking, delicious lunch specials and the best coffee in town. *Jl. Dewi Sita (next to the football pitch) | tel. 0361 97 57 54 | Moderate*

SHOPPING

Ubud has a wealth of boutiques and souvenir shops. You can buy everything you need – from groceries to souvenirs – every day at the *Pasar Ubud (junction of Jl. Raya Ubud/Monkey Forest Road)*. Be sure to use all your bargaining skills! An ☺ organic farmers' market is held every Saturday in front of *Pizza Bagus (10am–2pm | Jl. Raya Pengosekan)*.

There are many villages where handicrafts are produced in the area around Ubud: *Mas* is renowned for its woodcarvers, *Penestanan* for paintings and *Peliatan* for shadow theatre marionettes. The best stonemasons work a little further away in *Batubulan* and *Celuk* is the place to go to buy reasonably-priced silver items.

BALI BUDDHA ☺
Popular organic food shop with its own bakery, café and delivery service. *Jl. Jembawan 1*

STUDIO PERAK
Novel silver jewellery at reasonable prices; the owners also give silversmith courses. *Jl. Hanoman | www.studioperak.com*

THREADS OF LIFE
The Indonesian Textile Art Center promotes and sells traditional woven art from various sections of the country. *Jl. Kajeng 24 | www.threadsoflife.com*

UTAMA SPICE ☺
Organic tea and natural cosmetics produced according to old Balinese recipes. *Jl. Monkey Forest | www.utamaspicebali. com*

SPORTS & ACTIVITIES

Ubud is the ideal starting point for tours to explore the surrounding countryside: rice field hikes and bicycle tours are organised by *Bali Budaya Tours (tel. 0361 97 55 57 | www.baliecocycling.com)*. The birdwatching hikes with the ornithologist *Victor Mason (tel. 0361 97 50 09 | www. balibirdwalk.com)* have become legendary and the medicinal herb strolls *(Herbal Walks | tel. 0812 3 81 60 24 | baliherbalwalk. com)* are also very interesting.

Spas are an important part of Ubud: there is a great variety of affordable spa

VOLCANOES

There are 128 active volcanoes in Indonesia and 65 of them are considered dangerous. The more than 17,000 islands of the archipelago lie like a string of pearls on the Pacific Ring of Fire where three tectonic plates collide, often resulting in earthquakes. The highest mountain on Bali, the Gunung Agung 3148m (10,328ft) was believed to be extinct but erupted most recently in 1963 killing over a thousand people. The smaller Gunung Batur is also still active. The Gunung Rinjani (3726m/12,224ft) on Lombok is the second highest volcano in the country. Nobody was injured when it last erupted in 1994.

treatments from the *Sang Spa I and III (Jl. Jembawan 29b and Jl. Monkey Forest | tel. 0361 8 63 18 16 and 9 27 73 33)*; Taksu *(Jl. Gootama Selatan 35 | tel. 0361 97 14 90 | www.taksuspa.com)* offers a holistic approach and a panoramic view of the jungle. Yoga and meditation courses are offered everywhere; two that can be recommended are the *Yoga Barn (Jl. Pengosekan | Padang Tegal | tel. 0361 97 12 36 | www.theyogabarn.com)* and the small yoga and meditation centre ● *White Lotus (Jl. Kajeng 23 | tel. 0899 0 13 49 62 | sandeh-goeb@hotmail.com)* where it is possible to have a private yoga holiday without any kind of group pressure. The ● *ARMA Museum (see: Sightseeing, tel. 0361 97 66 59)* and *Bali Spirit (Jl. Hanoman | tel. 0361 97 09 92 | www.balispirit.com)* organise interesting courses in Balinese dance, gamelan and handicrafts. Traditional dance and music performances are held every evening in and around Ubud; the *Ubud Tourist Information* will provide you with the current events.

ENTERTAINMENT

JAZZ CAFE

Live bands play jazz, Latin and soul music every evening. *Tue–Sun 5pm–midnight | Jl. Sukma 2 | tel. 0361 97 65 94*

LAUGHING BUDDHA BAR

Exotic cocktails, fabulous live bands and a marvellous atmosphere. *Tue–Sun 4pm–midnight | Jl. Monkey Forest (opposite Cafe Wayan) | tel. 0361 97 09 28*

XL SHISHA LOUNGE

Hookahs and belly dancers in a Middle Eastern décor; live music in the evening. *Daily 3pm–2am | Jl. Monkey Forest (behind the football pitch) | tel. 0361 97 57 51*

WHERE TO STAY

ALAM INDAH

Bright rooms in Balinese style overlooking the Wo River valley. Pool, spa and garden. *10 rooms | Nyuhkuning | tel. 0361 97 46 29 | www.alamindahbali.com | Moderate*

Nightlife in Ubud is pulsating and sometimes even rather sophisticated

GUCI GUESTHOUSE
Artist homestay in a quiet location with large bungalows in a beautiful garden, duplex with kitchen for families; very friendly service. *5 rooms| Jl. Raya Pengosekan | tel. 0361 97 59 75 | www.guci-bali.com | Budget*

KAJANE 😊
The luxurious, beautifully landscaped villa resort with pool, natural spa and organic restaurant is in the very heart of town. *40 rooms, 8 villas | Jl. Monkey Forest | tel. 0361 97 28 77 | www.kajane.com | Expensive*

KENANGA BOUTIQUE HOTEL ᛌᛚ 😊
Chic, contemporary hotel with a fantastic view of the rice terraces outside of Ubud. Restaurant, gigantic pool and spa where you can have treatments with products made on the premises. *15 rooms | Jl. Lungsiakan | tel. 0361 8 98 97 00 | www.kenangaubud.com | Expensive*

KETUT'S PLACE
Family hotel with lovely garden that overlooks the valley, pool and spa. If requested in advance, the owners will make a delicious Balinese buffet meal. *17 rooms | Jl. Suweta 40 | tel. 0361 97 53 04 | www.ketutsplace.com | Budget–Moderate*

INSIDER TIP ▸ VILLA PECATU
The five modern apartments, each with a large terrace and private kitchen, are located right next to a rice field. *Jl. Pengosekan (opposite Panorama Hotel) | tel. 0361 97 13 83 | www.geocities.jp/villapecatupengosekan | Moderate*

TJAMPUHAN HOTEL ᛌᛚ
The former home of the painter Walter Spies forms part of the elegant, historic hotel that has two swimming pools and a spa. With a view of a canyon. *67 rooms |*
Jl. Raya Campuan | tel. 0361 97 53 68 | www.tjampuhan-bali.com | Expensive

UBUD SARI HEALTH RESORT 😊
This wellness resort boasts 15 traditional bungalows in a magnificently landscaped garden; pool, natural spa and organic restaurant. Detox and cleansing treatments. *Jl. Kajeng 35 | tel. 0361 97 43 93 | www.ubudsari.com | Moderate*

INFORMATION

UBUD TOURIST INFORMATION
Jl. Raya Ubud (opposite Ubud Palace) | tel. 0361 97 32 85

LOW BUDGET

▶ Most of the dance and music performance at the *Bali Arts Festival* (June/July) in Denpasar are free and there is much more variety than in the normal shows for tourists.

▶ You can have an excellent massage without any fancy extras for as little as 150,000 Rp (90 minutes) in the *Cozy Spa (Jl. Sunset Blok A3 | Legian | tel. 0361 76 67 62)* in Seminyak.

▶ ● Instead of paying the fee to use a *sarong* and sash when you visit the temples on Bali, buy your own inexpensive wrap-around at the start of your holiday and always have it with you.

▶ If you make several trips with the shuttle buses of *Perama Tours (www.peramatour.com)*, you will be given a discount upon presentation of the old tickets.

Everyday life at the crater lake in front of the majestic Gunung Batur

WHERE TO GO

GOA GAJAH ᰔ (135 D2) (∅ K5)
Southeast of Ubud (2km/1.2mi) steep steps leads up to the so-called Elephant Cave from the 9th century. One enters the interior with a statue of the god Ganesha – half man, half elephant – through the mouth of a demon. The Dutch came across the cave in 1923 and the sacred spring with the two rectangular bathing places in front of it was discovered 30 years later. You should try to arrive here as early as possible in order to avoid the tour groups. *Daily 8am–5pm | entrance fee 15,000 Rp.*

GUNUNG BATUR ★ ᰔ
(132 A–B 2–3) (∅ L2–3)
If you want to experience sunrise on the summit of the Gunung Batur (1717m/5633ft, 45km/28mi northeast), you will have to get up early in the morning and climb in the dark up a stony path for around two hours – but it is well worth the effort as the view over the volcanic landscape is breathtaking. There are several routes and tours are arranged by *Bali Budaya Tours (tel. 0361 97 55 57 | www.bali ecocycling.com)* and other organisations. The view from ᰔ *Penelokan* (around 30km/19mi north of Ubud) is no less impressive and getting there is considerably less strenuous. With a length of 8km (5mi), Bali's largest crater lake *Danau Batur* takes up about one third of the inner caldera 500m (1640ft) below the crater rim. The *Pura Ulun Danu Batur* temple is dedicated to the goddess of the lake and was moved from the northern edge to a higher location after an earthquake in 1926.

The Bali Aga village *Trunyan,* on the eastern side can be reached by boat from Kedisan. The people living there do not bury their dead but lay them out under bamboo frames in the cemetery. They are suspicious of strangers and it is advisable to only visit in the company of a good guide.

GUNUNG KAWI ᰔ (135 E1) (∅ K4)
A long stairway hewn into the rocks leads into a fertile valley 20km (12mi) north of Ubud. Here, you will discover nine 7m (23ft) high niches in the rocks with carved shrines that supposedly date back to the

11th century. It is believed that the tombs of King Anak Wungsu and his family are behind them. According to the legend, the giant Kebo Iwa scratched them out of the rock. There is a tenth statue further down on the other side of the river where a former Buddhist monastery is also located. *Daily 8am–5pm | entrance fee 15,000 Rp.*

PEJENG (125 D2) (*∅ K5*)

One of Bali's six holiest temples, the *Pura Pusering Jagat* ('Temple at the Navel of the World'), where mainly young couples pray to be blessed with offspring, lies exactly in the middle of Bali is in the centre of the old Pejeng Empire, 3km (2mi) east of Ubud. 300m (984ft) further on, you can see the world's largest bronze drum and most important find from the Indonesian Bronze Age, the 'Moon of Pejeng', in the *Pura Penataran Sasih*. The nearby archaeological museum, *Gedung Arca Museum Arkeologi (Sat–Thu 8am–3pm, Fri 8am–noon | free admission),* has a display of artefacts that are over 2000 years old, diagonally across from the *Pura Kebo Edan*, the 'Temple of the Mad Buffalo', that is

famous for a 3.60m (12ft) high statue of Shiva. Today, the descendants of the king run a batik manufacture in the old palace *Puri Pejeng* to support the village (☺ **INSIDER TIP** *BISA Organic Batik | tel. 0813 37 33 09 44 | www.indigobatik.com).* The dyes necessary for the work are made using plants from the palace garden.

TIRTA EMPUL (135 E1) (*∅ K4*)

The Balinese have made pilgrimages to the sacred springs (25km/16mi north of Ubud), which – it is said – the Hindu god Indra invested with magical powers, for more than 1000 years. The clear water bubbles out of twelve carved fountains into the main pool and there are two smaller pools fed by the spring further down. *Daily 8am–5pm | entrance fee 15,000 Rp.*

YEH PULU (135 D2) (*∅ K5*)

A path along a brook leads to the *stone reliefs* near a sacred spring 2km (1.2mi) to the east of Ubud. The reliefs from the 14th century were discovered in 1925 but there is still some uncertainty over their meaning. *Daily 8am–5pm | entrance fee 15,000 Rp.*

Gunung Kawi: temple complex and burial site in the middle of the jungle

LOMBOK

For a long time, Lombok was over-shadowed by its neighbouring island Bali, but in recent years an increasing number of tourists have become interested in what is one of Indonesia's most fascinating islands: this is where Islam and Hinduism meet, where traditional and modern life rub shoulders, and where tropical rainforests and Austronesia savannahs merge.

Lombok (Indonesian for 'chilli') is dominated by the majestic massif of the 3726m (12,224 ft) high volcano Mount Rinjani, which covers the northern half of the island. Here, fertile rice terraces, palm groves and forests populated by monkeys and other wild animals make their way up the steep mountain slopes. The gigantic crater lake is held sacred for both the Muslim Sasak, Lombok's indigenous population, and Balinese Hindus and is one of the main attractions for tourists. In the arid south picturesque bays and coral reefs (with perfect conditions for surfers and divers) lie hidden between cliffs in front of the hilly savannah landscape. The 1824 square mile large island has the Wallace Line to thank for its overwhelming biodiversity: the border between the Asian and Australian primeval continent ran through the 40km (25mi) wide and up to 3000m (9843ft) deep ocean trench between

Island of great diversity: luxuriant nature and cultural contrasts make Lombok a fascinating travel destination for explorers

Lombok and Bali. The flora and fauna of Southeast Asia and Austronesia have mixed here over thousands of years. Lombok is more unspoilt, more natural than Bali; but, it is also harsher. The more than 3 million inhabitants live mainly from agriculture and only the western section of the island has been really developed for tourism. The Sasak people are devout Muslims, they value modesty and have conservative views about alcohol consumption, especially outside of the tourist resorts. The villages in the east, in particular, are often dominated by outsized mosques. In spite of that, Hindu and animist customs have found their way into Islam as it practiced here – especially by the followers of the Wetu Telu faith ('three elements') in the north of the island who see themselves as the

Outrigger boats are still used to fish off of Kuta's coast

descendants of the first Islam preacher on Lombok. They only pray three times a day and fast for a mere three days during Ramadan. However, out of fear of being discriminated against, very few openly profess their faith. A Hindu minority lives in the west; they are the descendants of the Balinese rulers who conquered Lombok in the 17th century before being driven out themselves by the Dutch at the end on the 19th century. Some temples and palaces around the capital city Mataram still bear witness to this period.

Lombok was considered an insider tip for a long time. However, with the opening of the new international airport only a few miles north of Kuta, at the latest, a new wave of tourism – promoted by the government campaign 'Visit Lombok Sumbawa' – started on the island. Numerous new villa complexes and resorts have already been opened in Senggigi. However, the investors have focused their interest on the previously unspoilt south of the island: especially in the area around Kuta, many large projects are planned including the Mandalika Resorts Project, which will ultimately stretch for 7.5km (5mi) from Kuta to Gerupuk. In spite of that, Lombok – with its huge mountains, countless bays and dozens of lesser-known *gilis* ('small islands') – has remained a paradise for tourists who want to discover new places.

KUTA

(136 C5) (*ⁿ R9*) **Unlike Bali's Kuta, this small fishing village on the south coast of Lombok is very peaceful.**

When the shrimp boats set out to sea with their nets in the twilight, their lights cast a romantic glow over the entire bay. The restaurants and guesthouses that line the main street are all rather simple; the only luxury accommodation available is 3km (2mi) out of town. This will probably all change soon; numerous investors announced construction projects after the international airport was opened only 25km (16mi) north of Kuta. So far, mainly backpackers and surfers have found their way to Kuta – it is the best starting point for exploring the spectacular ★ *south-coast of Lombok*: the coast road winds its way past wild hills and rugged cliffs with still more beautiful bays and secluded beaches, the further one travels.

With the exception of some moped riders, the only people on the road are farmers in their buffalo-drawn wagons; some of them still live in traditional Sasak villages such as *Rambitan* and *Sade* in the south. At the time of the full moon in February/March, they all congregate on Kuta's beaches to celebrate the Bau Nyale Festival when they catch Nyale worms between the coral and then fry and eat them. There is also a great deal of flirting at this fertility ritual.

FOOD & DRINK

Most of the places offering accommodation also have a café or restaurant.

ASHTARI ● ☼

Cosy, oriental style vegetarian restaurant located on a hill to the west of Kuta with a fantastic view of the bay. *Only open during the day | Jl. Raya Kuta-Mawun | tel. 0817 5 78 75 02 | Budget*

FULL MOON CAFE

Delicious seafood and fresh juice are served in simple bamboo huts directly on the beach. *At the eastern end of Jl. Raya Pantai Kuta | tel. 0818 03 63 41 71 | Budget*

SPORTS & ACTIVITIES

Most people who spend any time in Kuta want to go surfing. The most popular bays for this sport are *Mawi* in the west and *Gerupuk* and *Tanjung Aan* in the east. *Kimen Surf (Jl. Raya Kuta | Mawun | tel. 0370 6 15 50 64 | kimensurf@kuta-lombok.net)* organises equipment, courses and tours to more distant surf spots. Diving courses and tours to the less visited, but spectacular, diving spots in the south of Lombok are offered *Divezone (Jl. Raya Kuta | tel. 0370 6 60 32 05 | www.divezone-lombok.com)*.

BEACHES

The many local activities make Kuta's beach itself not especially inviting but there is an ideal bathing beach 10km (6mi) west of the town in the beautiful curved bay at *Mawun*. Further to the west, follow the road past the surfing beach at *Mawi* until you arrive at the bay at INSIDER TIP *Selong Belanak,* with its breathtaking panorama of the cliffs at sunset. If you want to enjoy this spectacle for longer, you can spend the night in the very beautiful ᐳᐸ *Sempiak Villas (3 villas| tel. 0821 7 44 30 33 37 | www.sempiakvillas.com | Moderate)* – or just have a delicious dinner in the complex's *Laut Biru Cafe*. The sheltered sandy beach at *Tanjung Aan* around 7km (4mi) east of Kuta is ideal for swimming and surfing. A further 3km (2mi) to the east, you reach *Gerupuk Bay,* which is very popular with surfers.

WHERE TO STAY

KUTA PARADISE

Six unpretentious, modern bungalows around a pool; also a simple restaurant. At the eastern end of the main street. *Jl. Pariwisata Pantai Kuta | tel. 0370 65 48 49 | Budget*

NOVOTEL LOMBOK ᐳᐸ ☺

Luxury Sasak style resort 3km (2mi) east of the village that supports a variety of environmental projects. Two pools, a spa, a restaurant, leisure activities and children's entertainment; all right on a picture-perfect beach. *102 rooms | Pantai Putri Nyale | tel. 0370 6 15 33 33 | www. novotel-lombok.com | Expensive*

SURFER'S INN

Unusual bungalow complex around a chic swimming pool; very clean. *25 rooms | Jl.*

The low-slung, grass-covered roofs are typical of Sasak architecture

Raya Pantai Kuta | tel. 0370 6 15 55 82 |
www.lombok-surfersinn.com | *Budget*

INSIDER TIP YULI'S HOMESTAY
Spotlessly clean child-friendly facility with
eight bungalows and two pools in a beautiful garden; shared kitchen. Very pleasant hosts. *In the centre of the village,
north of the main junction | tel. 0819
17 10 09 83 | www.yulishomestay.com |
Budget*

WHERE TO GO

EKAS BAY ⚹ (137 D–E5) (*ⓜ S9*)
This bay in the southeast of Lombok is
hardly developed for tourism, but has
some of the island's very best spots for
surfing, diving and snorkelling. After leaving Kuta, drive for around 25km (16mi)
to the fishing village of Awang and then
take a boat to the other side. For a longer stay you can book into the eco-resort
☺ **INSIDER TIP** *Heaven on the Planet
(5 chalets | tel. 0812 37 97 48 46 | www.
heavenontheplanet.co.nz/accommoda-
tion | Moderate)* in a spectacular location
on the cliffs. An alternative route is over
a bumpy road to the east.

RAMBITAN AND SADE ★
(137 D5) (*ⓜ R–S9*)
The traditional Sasak villages of Rambitan
and Sade are just 6km (4mi) north of Kuta.
The houses are built of clay and wood and
roofed with grass; in between, you will see
the rice granaries *(lumbung)* with their low
slung, bulbous roofs of palm leaves that
have served as models for countless bungalow resorts. Although these two villages
cater to tourists, it is still interesting to get
and insight into traditional village life. You
should not let them wheedle too much
money out of you for souvenirs and guide
fees; usually, a single donation at the
entrance to the village is enough.

CITY WHERE TO START?
Mataram Mall: About 200m
after you leave the mall on Jl.
Pejanggik you will reach the Rinjani
weaving mill on the other side of the
street. Turn to the left and after about
500m you will arrive at the Sindhu
market, continue straight ahead to
the Pura Meru and Mayura water
palaces (Jl. Selaparang). Buses leave
from here for the Mandalika market
at the Sweta bus terminus.

MATARAM

**(136 B3) (*ⓜ Q7*) Lombok's capital is a
conglomeration of four towns that have
now merged seamlessly into one and
have a population of half a million residents: the old port of Ampenan, Cakranegara with its Chinese character, the
small market town of Sweta, and
Mataram itself – a former royal city that
is now dominated by.**
Some temples and palaces still bear witness
to past glory. *Mataram* and *Cakranegara*,
with their business and shopping centres,
form the bustling centre of the island. The
former Dutch commercial port *Ampenan*
is mainly used by fishing boats today. A
main thoroughfare runs from there as far
as *Sweta;* all of the addresses that are of
interest to tourists can be found nearby.
Most visitors merely pass through the
town – but anybody interested in the
everyday life in an Indonesian provincial
town should make an excursion here.

SIGHTSEEING

MAYURA WATER PALACE
The 'floating pavilion' was erected in the
middle of a lotus pond in 1744. It served as

a court hall during the period of Balinese rule and this was where the Balinese fought against the Dutch at the end of the 19th century. Unfortunately, the remains of the complex were not maintained for many years and there were no renovations until 2012. The architectural melange of Hindu and Islamic elements, as well as the historical significance of the site – which only becomes clear to the layperson with the help of a knowledgeable guide *(set prices are displayed at the entrance)* – makes the water palace interesting for tourists. *Daily 7am–6pm | entrance fee 5000 Rp | Jl. Selaparang | Cakranegara*

MUSEUM NUSA TENGGARA BARAT ●

From wedding dresses, to shadow theatre puppets and daggers: you can learn a great deal about the culture and history of the Nusa Tenggara Barat province – Lombok and Sumbawa both belong to it – here. A translator (your driver or a guide) can be helpful. *Tue–Thu 8am–2pm, Fri 8am–11am, Sat 8am–12.30pm | entrance fee 5000 Rp | Jl. Panji Tilar Negara 6 | Mataram*

PURA MERU �►

A Balinese prince had the largest Hindu temple on Lombok built in 1720, in an attempt to unify the island's inhabitants. A path leads through two forecourts to an inner courtyard with 33 shrines. Three *meru* (pagodas), of different heights in a row, are dedicated to the three main Hindu deities Shiva, Brahma and Vishnu. The abandoned complex becomes overcrowded at the Pujawali festival held every year at full moon in October. *Daily 7am–6pm | admission for a donation | Jl. Selaparang | Cakranegara*

LOW BUDGET

▶ The trip between the new airport, Mataram and Senggigi is much cheaper with the *DAMRI Airport Bus* (25,000 Rp) than by taxi (165,000 Rp). However, the unreliable schedule makes this only advisable when you arrive.

▶ You can buy souvenirs considerably cheaper in Lombok's *handicraft villages* than at the markets or in shops.

▶ With the exception of Senggigi, wellness treatments are usually limited to spas in the major hotels and are correspondingly expensive. Most places offering accommodation are also able to arrange a private masseur on request (from 50,000 Rp per hour).

FOOD & DRINK

THE BERUGAQ ☺

Coffee, cakes and snacks are served along with the works of local artists in the attached gallery. The profits benefit the 'One Heart Foundation' that has the goal of improving medical care and education on Lombok. *Jl. Adi Sucipto | KP Griya Ellen Indah | Ampenan | tel. 0370 6 16 26 67 | Budget*

INSIDER TIP LESEHAN TALIWANG IRAMA ●

This restaurant is popular with the locals for its authentic Sasak cooking; it is said that this is the place to eat the best *Taliwang* chicken on Lombok. *Jl. Ade Irma Suryiani | Gang Salam 6 | Cakranegara | tel. 0370 62 31 63 | Budget*

SHOPPING

There are many small antique shops on *Jl. Saleh Sungkar* in Ampenan. Groceries,

There are no luxury brands in the Mataram Mall but all of the daily necessities

cosmetics and electrical appliances can be bought in the *Mataram Mall* and at other places. The largest traditional market on Lombok is right next to the Mandalika bus terminus in *Sweta*.

LOMBOK HANDICRAFT CENTER
Textiles, wood carvings, ceramics and basketwork from eastern Indonesia. *Jl. Hasanudin | Sayang-Sayang | Lingsar*

TENUN IKAT RINJANI HANDWOVEN
Traditional woven goods and clothing; you can watch the weavers at work in the morning. *Jl. Pejanggik 44–46 | Mataram*

WHERE TO STAY

HOTEL SANTIKA LOMBOK
The most modern business hotel in town with restaurant, bar, pool and gym. *123 rooms | Jl. Pejanggik 32 | Mataram | tel. 0370 6 17 88 88 | www.santika.com/ santika-lombok | Moderate*

VILLA SAYANG BOUTIQUE RESORT ☆ ☺
Surrounded by rice fields overlooking the Rinjani, this resort is popular as a stopover for tourists travelling from the Gilis to the airport. Lovely pool and tour service; the restaurant serves dishes made with organic ingredients from the hotel garden. *13 cottages | Jl. Sonokeling | Lingsar | Mataram | tel. 0370 6 60 90 22 | www. villasayang-lombok.com | Moderate*

INFORMATION

WEST NUSA TENGGARA TOURISM OFFICE
Jl. Singosari 2 | Mataram | tel. 0370 63 17 30

WHERE TO GO

PURA LINGSAR
(136 C3) (⑭ R7)
A Hindu temple and a Wetu Telu mosque stand peacefully next to each other in

the largest temple complex 7km (4mi) east of Cakranegara. The main section was built in 1714. As soon as the rainy season begins, Hindus and Sasak compete in the playful ● *Perang Topat* ('Rice Cake War'). *Daily 7am–6pm | admission for a donation*

SURANADI
(136 C3) *(∅ R7)*

The refreshing climate in this small town, only 18km (11mi) away from Mataram, makes it a popular place for excursions. The *Pura Suranadi* is the oldest and most important Hindu temple on Lombok. It was supposedly founded in the 16th century by the same Hindu priest who had Bali's six most sacred temples erected. Sacred moray eels swim in the temple spring and there is a flying fox station in the nearby monkey forest. The colonial *Hotel Suranadi (26 rooms| tel. 0370 6 57 84 10 | www. suranadihotel.com | Budget)* has a pool fed with cool spring water *(entrance fee for non-residents 10,000 Rp)* that is very popular on weekends.

TAMAN NARMADA (136 C4) *(∅ R7)*

The Narmada Park (11km/7mi east of Mataram) was laid out in 1727 by the Balinese King Anak Agung Gede Ngurah in honour of the god Shiva. A pleasure garden modelled on the Rinjani volcano was created around the *Pura Kalasa* temple; the large pool represents the crater lake. This made it possible for the king to continue to make his ritual offerings at the sacred water after he had become too old to climb the Rinjani itself. The terrace-like gardens and *public swimming pool (Fri closed | 5000 Rp)* make the spacious complex a popular weekend destination for people from the city. *Daily 7am–5.30pm | entrance fee 10 000 Rp.*

TETEBATU ★ ● (137 D3) *(∅ S7)*

This small village at an altitude of 400m/1312ft (47km/29mi from Mataram) is surrounded by rice terraces that are used as tobacco fields in the dry season. The village's panorama and refreshing climate already made it a popular destination for excursions in the colonial era. Today, it is

Head-high tobacco plants in the fields near Tetebatu

mainly visited by day-trippers and back-packers hiking to the nearby *Joben* and *Jukut* waterfalls (around 2 hours) or just looking for peace and quiet. You can spend the night in the *Wisma Soedjono (tel. 0818 27 97 74 | www.wismasoedjono. com | Budget)*. The simple, colonial style guesthouse offers walks through the monkey forest close by and orchards where coffee, cocoa, vanilla and cloves grow. The handicrafts village of *Loyok,* which is famous for its wickerwork, is 10km (6mi) further to the south.

SEKOTONG

(136 B4) *(⌘ Q8)* ⭐ In spite of years of investment plans, the mountainous peninsula in the southwest of Lombok has remained little developed for tourism.
A winding road weaves its way through small Sasak villages along the north coast with more than a dozen — mostly uninhabited — islands out to sea: the 'secret' Gilis. The islets have white sandy beaches, colourful corals and crystal-clear water and are a paradise for snorkellers and divers. There is a very bumpy road to the extreme western point *Bangko-Bangko,* where the breakers roll to shore at Desert Point, which is so famous amongst surfers. *Teluk Mekaki* is the only accessible bay in the south. Some new resorts have opened on Sekotong in recent years, and more are planned. The people live their traditional lives of agriculture and gold prospecting. A pearl farm is in operation on *Gili Gede.* There are only a few shops; the daily market in *Pelangan* offers food and handicrafts.

SPORTS & ACTIVITIES

All the resorts organise snorkelling tours and professional diving tours and courses can be booked from INSIDER TIP *Divezone (tel. 0819 16 00 14 26 | www.divezone-lombok.com). Desert Point* near Bangko-Bangko is considered the best surfing spot on Lombok — some resorts organise trips. If you want to explore the mountains on a bicycle, contact *Mountain Bike Lombok (tel. 0819 99 09 71 26 | www.mountainbike lombok.com).*

WHERE TO STAY

COCOTINOS 😊
Chic boutique resort in a palm grove with a view of the Gilis; pool, spa, restaurant and dive school, natural building design and waste recycling. *23 rooms, 5 villas | Dusun Pandanan | Sekotong Barat | tel. 0819 07 97 24 01 | www.cocotinos-sekotong. com | Moderate*

GILI NANGGU COTTAGES
Simple bungalow resort that has an entire island to itself. Restaurant, sports, family activities, turtle station. *17 rooms | Gili Nanggu | tel. 0370 62 37 83 | www. gilinanggu.com | Budget*

INSIDER TIP PEARL BEACH RESORT
Idyllic island resort at a former pearl farm; restaurant, spa and dive school. *10 bungalows | Gili Asahan | tel. 0819 0 72 47 69 | www.pearlbeach-resort.com | Budget*

SENARU

(137 D2) *(⌘ S6)* The small village on the slopes of the Rinjani is picturesquely nestled between lush rice terrace, flowering gardens and palm groves and is the most important starting point for climbs up the majestic volcano.
Those who don't want to tackle the multi-day climb to the summit can relax and enjoy the fresh air and fantastic views by

undertaking short excursions through the rice fields and rainforests to thundering waterfalls, or become acquainted with the traditional way of life of the villagers.

SPORTS & ACTIVITIES

Most of the tourists who come to Senaru aim to climb the Rinjani. Depending on the route, the hike takes three to four days and should never be undertaken without a professional guide. The ascent is usually too dangerous during the rainy season – and, of course, this is also true if the volcano is too active. The tours are organised centrally by *Rinjani Trek Ecotourism (Senaru/Senggigi/Sembalun/Mataram | tel. 0370 64 11 24 | www.lombokrinjanitrek.org)* whose office is located at the upper end of Senaru at the entrance to the national park. This is where all of the professional trekking operators that work together with the national park and village administration are registered *(such as John's Adventures | tel. 0817 5 78 80 18 | www.rinjanimaster.com and Restu By View | tel. 0817 5 73 77 51 | rinjanirestu @gmail.com).* Most accommodation in Senaru will help their guests to arrange a hike *(cost: around 3,000,000 Rp per person – the larger the group, the cheaper the price).*

WHERE TO STAY

Most of the places providing accommodation also have small restaurants.

HORIZON VILLA ⚘
Simple holiday villa with two bedrooms, a living room and veranda with spectacular views over the valley and to the Rinjani; ideal for families. *Jl. Raya Senaru (below the waterfall) | www.horizonsenaru.com | Budget*

RINJANI LIGHT HOUSE ☺
A wooden house on stilts just before the entrance to the national park, they offer fresh local food in the adjacent *warung* and support the women's mountain guide organisation. *4 rooms, 1 family cottage | Jl. Pariwisata Senaru (near the entrance to the national park) | tel. 0878 64 24 19 41 | rinjanilighthouse@gmail.com | Budget*

INSIDER TIP ▶ RINJANI MOUNTAIN GARDEN ⚘ ☺
This eco-resort with its luxuriant garden, natural swimming pool and all kinds of animals is located on the eastern side of the Senaru Valley high up on the slopes of the Rinjani. You can enjoy the fantastic views over rice terraces and coconut plantations all the way down to the ocean while savouring a delicious meal of Indonesian and European specialties in the restaurant, as well as undertake trekking and horseback tours. Those who do not want to spend the night in a hired tent can stay in one of the six pretty rice-granary style cottages. The electricity is generated by hydropower. *Teres Genit | Bayan | tel. 0818 56 97 30 | Budget*

WHERE TO GO

BAYAN
(137 D2) (*ᗑ S6*)
The main village of the Wetu Telu followers is 6km (4mi) north of Senaru and is the site of the oldest mosque on the island. Built from bamboo and clay it is 300 years old. The inhabitants of Bayan regard themselves as direct descendants of the holy man who is said to have brought Islam to the island in the 16th century and they have continued to maintain a mixture of animistic, Hindu and Islamic traditions to the present day. For a small donation, the mosque guardian will be delighted to

The turquoise waters of the sacred lake, the Segara Anak, glistening in the crater of the Gunung Rinjani

tell you the history of the village. However, you will have to rely on the translation skills of your driver if you want to understand him.

DUSUN SENARU AND SEGENTER
(137 D1–2) (*∅ S6*)

The unspoilt village of *Senaru* is at the upper end of the modern town: the people here still live as they did hundreds of years ago in communal bamboo houses with clay floors. The architectural style, language and traditions differ from those of the Sasak in the south. Visitors who make a small donation at the entrance to the village will be shown the traditional way of life. Around 12km (8mi) north on the road to Senggigi, there is a signpost pointing to *Segenter,* another completely preserved Sasak village.

GUNUNG RINJANI ★
(137 D–E2) (*∅ R–T 6–7*)

Its height of 3726m (12,224ft) makes the Rinjani the second highest volcano in

Indonesia and its majestic massif covers around half of the surface of Lombok. The *Segara Anak* ('Child of the Sea') lake in its gigantic crater is up to 6km (4mi) wide and is considered sacred by both the Sasak and Hindus on Lombok. The active *Gunung Baru,* which was created following a powerful eruption of the mother volcano, towers up next to it. Nobody suffered injuries when it last erupted in 2010. The ● *Rinjani National Park (entrance fee 150,000 Rp)* covers 101,313 acres of lush rainforest and bizarre volcanic landscapes and is the home of unique flora and fauna: wild boar, dwarf deer and giant lizards, as well as rare birds, butterflies and plants. After you start your ascent at Sena, you will pass caves and hot springs that the local people believe have magical powers. There is an additional entrance to the national park in Sembalun Lawang in the east. On no account should you attempt to climb the mountain on your own. Despite warning there are always some stubborn tourists who do so and end up

The Sindanggila Waterfall cascades down to the valley from the slopes of the Gunung Rinjani

getting lost in the wilderness, injure themselves or even perish. The increasing number of trekking tours has led to the introduction of a zero-waste programme in which the bearers are paid an extra sum for the rubbish they bring down from the mountain.

SINDANGGILA AND TIU KELEP WATERFALL (137 D2) (*∅ S6*)

Around 1.5km (1mi) from Senaru the picturesque Sindanggila Waterfall plummets thunderously down into the valley over two cascades. The footpath from the main road *(next to the Pondok Senaru Restaurant / entrance fee 5000 Rp)* is well developed and the walk takes around 20 minutes. People are usually accompanied by a guide (do not pay more than noted on the sign at the entrance). A real professional is only required if you want to continue your climb up to the Tiu Kelep Waterfall: a steep, slippery path leads to a natural swimming pool in around three quarters of an hour.

SENGGIGI

(136 B3) (*∅ Q7*) This former fishing village (pop. 9000) in the west of Lombok has now spread out over several beautiful, curved bays – and there is no sign of the building work stopping.

The white sand beaches – from where you can see as far as Bali's majestic Gunung Agung at sunset on a clear day – make the place an ideal holiday destination. Of course, the strategic location, between the ferry harbour in Labuhan Lembar, the old airport at Ampenan and the Gilis in the northwest, has also helped Senggigi's development into Lombok's most important tourist destination. This is the perfect starting point to explore Lombok from the land or water. Although there are now restaurants and places offering accommodation in all price categories, Senggigi has remained very peaceful and inexpensive when compared with the tourist centres on Bali.

SIGHTSEEING

If you drive along the road from Ampenan to Senggigi, you will come across a small Hindu temple, the ⚡ *Pura Batu Bolong (daily 7am–7pm)* on some rocks above the bay of the same name. The temple is dedicated to Brahma, the god of creation, and there is an empty throne waiting for his arrival. The Hindus from western Lombok come here especially for the full moon ceremonies. It is only a short distance from here to the next rock, the *Batu Layar,* with the tomb of the Muslim saint Syeh Syayid Muhammad al Bagdadi who is said to have brought Islam to Lombok.

FOOD & DRINK

Most of the restaurants provide a shuttle service to and from the hotels outside of town.

ASMARA

Whether you choose Sasak specialities, pasta or steak, this is one of the best classic style restaurants in town; also special meals for children and a corner for them to play in. *Jl. Raya Senggigi | tel. 0370 69 36 19 | Moderate*

BIG BLUE

A beach lounge serving cocktails and international cuisine along with cool music next to the pool. *Art Market | Jl. Raya Senggigi | tel. 0877 63 03 53 36 | Moderate*

INSIDER TIP COCO BEACH ☺

There are a handful of *berugaqs* (covered pavilions for sitting) around a beach bar in the coconut grove north of Senggigi where organic food from their own garden and fresh drinks are served. An ideal place to relax! *Pantai Kerandangan | Pintu 2 | tel. 0817 5 78 00 55 | Budget*

DE QUAKE

Sophisticated seafood creations and cocktails are served in this simply decorated restaurant on the beach behind the art market. *Art Market | Jl. Raya Senggigi | tel. 0370 69 36 94 | Moderate*

SQUARE

Probably the trendiest restaurant in Senggigi, with one of the best chefs from Bali. In the lounge on the first floor there is late night club music. *Jl. Raya Senggigi 8km | tel. 0370 6 64 59 99 | Expensive*

TAMAN RESTAURANT

International cuisine from Australia to India, and frequent live music performances; the attached bakery makes it a good place for breakfast. *Jl. Raya Senggigi | tel. 0370 69 38 42 | Moderate*

SHOPPING

There are hawkers everywhere on the beach during the day. Products from all over Lombok can be found at the *art market (pasar seni)* at the northern end of town. The small shops in the centre of Senggigi sell food, cosmetics and other daily needs.

ASMARA ART SHOP

The shop in front of the eponymous restaurant sells lovely fabrics and high-quality handicrafts. *Jl. Raya Senggigi | www. asmara-group.com*

AUTORE PEARL CULTURE

One of Lombok's largest pearl farms; all of the pearls sold have a certificate of authenticity. Tours are also organised. *Teluk Nare | www.pearlautore.com*

SPORTS & ACTIVITIES

Almost all of the dive organisations have offices in Senggigi. Dive courses can be booked from *Dream Divers (Jl. Raya Senggigi kav. 15 | tel. 0370 69 37 38 | www.dreamdivers-lombok.com)*.

The *Rinjani Trekking Club (tel. 0370 69 32 02 | www.rinjanitrekclub.org)* can provide information for those who want to climb the Rinjani. *E-one Tours & Travel (Jl. Raya Senggigi (in front of the Asmara Artshop) | tel. 0370 69 38 43 | www.lomboktoursandtravel.com)* is a reliable vehicle rental company and also organises excursions.

Relax in the spas in the large hotels: the treatments in the *Sheraton Senggigi Beach (Jl. Raya Senggigi | tel. 0370 69 33 33)* are especially recommended. Another place for very good – and much less expensive – massages is the simple *Arirang Lombok Salon & Spa (Jl. Senggigi Plaza Block C-1 | tel. 0370 6 19 42 72)*.

BEACHES

Senggigi's main beach is full of small kiosks, hawkers and fishing and excursion boats. The Senggigi Beach Hotel rents deckchairs for 30,000 Rp – they are particularly popular at the sunset happy hour when there is also live music. The best place for swimming is at the beach in front of the Café Alberto in *Batu Bolong*. The beautiful beach at *Mangsit* has now been taken over by hotels but there are still peaceful stretches of beach lined with palm trees in *Klui, Malimba* and *Nipah* Bays.

WHERE TO STAY

THE CHANDI

The boutique resort is located on the tranquil beach at Batu Layar. Restaurant, beach bar, pool and spa. *17 bungalows | Jl. Raya Senggigi | Batu Bolong | tel. 0370 69 21 98 | www.the-chandi.com | Expensive*

JEEVA KLUI

A spacious, understated boutique hotel with a natural design has a chic restaurant and pool and is right on the tranquil beach at Klui. *35 suites | Jl. Raya Klui 1 | tel. 0370 69 30 35 | jeevaklui.com | Expensive*

Simple but functional: outrigger boats on the beach at Senggigi

INSIDER TIP THE PUNCAK 🌤

Very friendly boutique hotel high up on 'The Hill', an exclusive villa district above Senggigi; fabulous view. *5 rooms | The Hill | Batu Layar | tel. 0821 11 13 95 95 | www.thepuncak.com | Expensive*

QUNCI VILLAS

Chic, modern boutique hotel with three pools directly on the beach, spa. Two excellent restaurants serving Asian and Western fusion cuisine and a beach bar. *80 rooms | Jl. Raya Mangsit | tel. 0370 69 38 00 | www.quncivillas.com | Expensive*

SANTAI BEACH INN ☺

This small Sasak style bungalow resort with a luxuriant garden on the seafront seems to be a remnant of former hippie days. Guests feel like members of the family when they take their meals together. Ecological concept. *10 bungalows | Jl. Raya Mangsit | tel. 0370 69 30 38 | www.santaibeachinn.com | Budget*

SENDOK GUEST HOUSE

Charming budget hotel in the centre of town with a small pool and restaurant. *18 rooms | Jl. Raya Senggigi 8km | tel. 0370 69 31 76 | www.sendok-bali.com/sendok 2g.htm | Budget*

SENGGIGI BEACH HOTEL

Lavish hotel complex on Senggigi's most central beach. Three restaurants, two bars, large pool and sports facilities. The hotel's exclusive Pool Villa Club has 16 two-storey villas with private Jacuzzi and pool access. *150 rooms | Jl. Pantai Senggigi | tel. 0370 69 32 10 | senggigibeachhotel. com | Moderate–Expensive*

SUNSETHOUSE

Modern, small hotel right on the lovely beach at Batu Bolong; with pool and lovely Sunset Bar. *20 rooms | Jl. Raya Senggigi 66 | Batu Bolong | tel. 0370 69 20 20 | www.sunsethouse-lombok. com | Moderate*

WHERE TO GO

BANYUMULEK AND SUKARARA ★ ●
(136 B–C4) (𝄢 Q–R8)

Around 24km (15mi) from Senggigi is the pottery village of Banyumulek famous for its earthenware with simple designs. The pottery is now exported worldwide. In the morning, visitors can watch the potters firing their creations. The weaving centre Sukarara is about 15km (9mi) further to the southeast. The women sit in front of their houses, with their legs stretched out in front of them, weaving at their looms. The elaborate fabrics are sold in the shop run by the village collective.

GUNUNG PENGSONG 🌤
(136 B4) (𝄢 Q8)

An enchanted 16th century Hindu temple on a hill 27km (17mi) from Senggigi that is populated by a band of cheeky monkeys. From here, you will have a wonderful panoramic view over West Lombok and – if the weather is fine – to the sea and the Rinjani. A buffalo is sacrificed here every year in March/April to invoke a good harvest. *Daily 7am–6pm | free admission*

TIU PUPUS AND KERTA GANGGA
(136 C2) (𝄢 R6)

The 50m (164ft) high *Tiu Pupus Waterfall* is 4.5km (3mi) south of Gondang (around 30km/19mi north of Senggigi). Although there is not much water in the dry season, it is still worth making the pleasant walk. It is twice the distance to the impressive double-cascade waterfall, the *Air Terjun Kerta Gangga,* with a bathing pool and caves. Both waterfalls can also be reached by car.

GILI ISLANDS

Strung like pearls in the glittering turquoise sea off the northwest coast of Lombok are Gili Air, Gili Meno and Gili Trawangan (simply called 'the Gilis') which just means 'small islands'.

They are a heaven on earth for snorkellers, divers and holidaymakers who just want to relax on the beach. All of the three islands have crystal-clear waters surrounded by coral reefs which you can access straight from the endless white ★ *beaches*. Most of the accommodation on the car-free islands are located on their peaceful eastern coasts and have spectacular views of the volcano Mount Rinjani. There are small bamboo pavilions *(berugak)* on the

beaches where holidaymakers can relax and enjoy exotic drinks and snacks.

In the 1980s, the first backpackers discovered the largely uninhabited Gilis where previously only a few fishermen from northern Sulawesi had planted some groves of coconut palms. Bamboo huts and hammocks gave them feel a Robinson Crusoe atmosphere. Today, around 3500 people live on the Gilis. The predominantly Muslim population is very tolerant, so you will have no trouble enjoying your holiday to the full – even during Ramadan – as long as certain fundamental rules (such as never sunbathing nude or topless) are observed.

Photo: Gili Meno

Coral reefs and bamboo bungalows in coconut groves form the perfect backdrop for a modern Robinson Crusoe holiday

Tourism only really took off in recent years when the government initiated a campaign and massive investments came from abroad. Thanks to this it is now possible to reach the Gilis directly from Bali. Since then, *Gili Trawangan* in particular has developed into a party island that some see to be a kind of Ibiza of the Far East. An increasing number of cafés, bars and chic resorts are also opening their doors on *Gili Air* but there are still many idyllic retreats from all the hustle and bustle. *Gili Meno*, on the other hand, has managed to preserve its peaceful 'get away from it all' atmosphere. Horse-drawn carriages and bicycles are the only means of transport on all three islands.

However, you will have to hire a boat if you want to explore the really beautiful snorkelling and diving areas in the ★ *underwater*

An Eldorado for divers just a short boat trip away from the Gilis

world off the Gilis because the corals close to the islands have been severely damaged by dynamite fishing. The Gili Eco Trust has been set up to attract to attract new corals on artificial reefs. Environmental awareness plays a major role on the small islands: for example, in order to avoid waste, the shops and cafés refill empty water bottles. Drinking water is scarce on the Gilis and the tap water is usually rather salty.

There are also no uniformed policemen on the islands – civil guards take care of security. There are now several ATMs on Gili Trawangan and one ATM to the east of the harbour jetty on Gili Air. Credit cards are only accepted in the larger hotels and restaurants, as well as by most of the dive organisers. It is only possible to convert currency with local money changers who charge high rates so it is a good idea to take sufficient cash. Small clinics provide basic medical care but, if you become seriously ill, you should return to Lombok

or Bali as soon as possible. There is mobile telephone reception and internet cafés on all three islands.

There are crossings to the Gilis from both Bali and Lombok *(speedboats from Benoa or Padang Bai | from US$45, 1.5 hours| gili-fastboat.com; from Senggigi with Perama Tour | 200,000 Rp, 30 minutes | www.peramatour.com)*. Inter-island shuttles and private motor boats depart from *Bangsal*.

GILI AIR

(139 D–F 4–6) *(𝄞 s–u 4–6)* **Those who don't feel like partying but still want to have some company will feel at home on Gili Air – families in particular enjoy this island.**

Gili Air (which means 'water island') is the closest to Lombok and, with around 1500 inhabitants, more densely populated than the other Gilis. The island is covered in coconut groves and there are mainly simple bungalow resorts and beach cafés but an increasing number of restaurants and resort style accommodations are opening. They can all be reached via the beach path – mostly unpaved – that runs around the island. The best place for swimming and snorkelling is in the southeast. There are only limited shopping possibilities.

FOOD & DRINK

BIBA BEACH CAFE (139 F5) (*ơ u5*)
Delicious pasta and wood-fired pizza in the Italian-run beach café that is part of the bungalow complex of the same name. *At the eastern beach | tel. 0370 17 27 46 48 | Budget*

INSIDER TIP ▶ GILI AIR SANTAY ☺
(139 F5) (*ơ u5*)
This is an institution on the island and is mainly famous for its Thai curries and shakes that are made exclusively with fresh, local products. One of the first restaurants with waste recycling. *In the northeast | tel. 0819 15 99 37 82 | www. giliair-santay.com | Budget*

MIRAGE BAR (139 E4) (*ơ t4*)
Mediterranean style cocktail bar; ideal for sundowners. *In the northwest near the Gili Air Hotel | Budget*

SPORTS & ACTIVITIES

Most of the places offering accommodation also organise snorkelling and fishing excursions and rent the necessary equipment. Professional dive courses and tours are offered by: *Dream Divers (tel. 0370 63 45 47 | www.dreamdivers-lombok. com | (139 F6) (*ơ u6*)), Blue Marlin Dive (tel. 0370 63 43 87 | www.bluemarlin dive.com | (139 F5) (*ơ u6*))* and the new

diving resort *Manta Dive (tel. 0813 37 78 90 47 | www.manta-dive-giliair.com | (139 F6) (*ơ u6*)).* In the centre of the island H_2O Yoga *(tel. 0877 61 03 88 36 | www.h2oyogaandmeditation.com | (139 E–F5) (*ơ t–u5*))* organise yoga courses and meditation retreats, as well as go, in the centre of the island.

WHERE TO STAY

VILLA CASA MIO (139 F4) (*ơ u4*)
Offbeat complex with four comfortable and colourfully decorated bungalows, pool and living room style beach café. *Southern west coast | tel. 0370 64 61 60 | www.giliair.com | Moderate*

COCONUT COTTAGES (139 F5) (*ơ u5*)
The 14 simple air-conditioned bungalows, with warm water, are tucked behind fran gipani trees, bougainvillea and hibiscus bushes and are only a short distance from the beach. Good garden restaurant. *Central east coast | tel. 0370 63 53 65 | www.coconuts-giliair.com | Budget*

★ **Beaches**
Relax in bamboo pavilions on the long white sandy beaches → p. 90

★ **Underwater world**
The corals, fish and sea turtles fascinate snorkellers and divers → p. 91

★ **Nightlife**
Whether in a cosy Irish pub or a cool lounge – party animals can celebrate all night on Trawangan → p. 95

MARCO POLO HIGHLIGHTS

INSIDER TIP▶ ISLAND VIEW
(139 F5) *(m u5)*

Six simple, but charming, bungalows in a tropical garden far away on the sunset side of the island; very nice beach café. *West coast | tel. 0878 64 94 21 26 | www.islandviewgiliair.com | Budget*

SUNRISE HOTEL (139 F6) *(m u6)*

268 granary style double-storey bunga-lows set in a lush garden; at the best spot for swimming on the east coast. *tel. 0370 64 23 70 | sunrisegiliair.com | Moderate*

GILI MENO

(139 D–F 1–3) *(m s–u 1–3)* **Gili Meno ('salt island') has a true Robinson Crusoe feel: it is the smallest and most peaceful of the three Gilis.**

You can walk around it in about ninety minutes. In the centre there is a *bird park (daily 9am–5pm | entrance fee 60,000 Rp* (139 E2) *(m t2))* with 300 different spe-cies of birds, as well as some crocodiles. The salt lake in the west gave the island its name and it is notorious for the mos-quitoes found there – especially at the end of the rainy season. They will not

affect your pleasure on the beach during the rest of the year. The loveliest spots for snorkelling are in the northwest, north-east and southeast of the island. On the main road in front of the Gazebo Hotel there is a *turtle station* that is open to the public and gives information about the endangered marine creatures.

FOOD & DRINK

INSIDER TIP▶ ADENG-ADENG BEACH BAR ☺ (139 E2) *(m t2)*

Romantic setting with delicious cocktails and tapas at sunset followed by a seafood barbecue by torch light. Environmentally conscious management. *At the northern end | tel. 0818 05 34 10 19 | Budget–Moderate*

MAHAMAYA BOUTIQUE RESORT RESTAURANT ● (139 D1) *(m s1)*

Chic beach restaurant at the eponymous boutique resort; fresh seafood, interna-tional and Indonesian cuisine. View of the setting sun. *North of the salt lake | tel. 0888 715 58 28 |Moderate*

TAO KOMBO RESTAURANT AND JUNGLE BAR (139 E3) *(m t3)*

Barbecue restaurant serving Indonesian and international food and the bar offers live music until late at night. *A short way inland at the southeast tip | tel. 0812 3 72 21 74 | Budget*

SPORTS & ACTIVITIES

The main attraction for snorkellers and divers is the *Gili Meno Wall*, with its rare corals, fish and sea turtles, in the north-west. All the dive centres on the Gilis offer tours to Gili Meno including *Blue Marlin Dive (tel. 0370 63 99 80 | www.bluemar-lindive.com | (139 F2–3) (m u2–3))* and

Divine Divers (tel. 0852 40 57 07 77 | www. divinedivers.com | (139 F2–3) (ⓜ u2–3)) on the island itself. Most of the places providing accommodation also organise snorkelling excursions, and yoga courses can be booked through *Mao Meno (www. mao-meno.com | (138 C4) (ⓜ r4)).*

VILLA NAUTILUS (139 F2–3) (ⓜ u2–3)
Five comfortable stone bungalows with air conditioning, warm water, sundeck and beach café. *In the southeast | tel. 0370 64 21 43 | www.villanautilus.com | Moderate*

SUNSET GECKO 😊 (139 D1) (ⓜ s1)
Six imaginatively decorated multi-room bungalows with an eco-friendly concept; right in front of a coral reef at the north-west beach. *Tel. 0813 53 56 07 74 | www. thesunsetgecko.com | Budget*

INSIDER TIP ▸ VILLA SAYANG
(139 E1) (ⓜ t1)
Three pleasantly decorated villas with separate living area, kitchen, open-air bath, and cleaning service in a spacious garden a little inland. Ideal for families. *North of the jetty | tel. 0370 6 60 90 01 | villasayanggilimeno.com | Moderate*

GILI TRAWANGAN

(138 A–C 2–5) (ⓜ p–r 2–5) **Gili Trawangan is the largest Gili and also the one most developed for tourism: hotels and restaurants in all price categories have opened here in recent years.**
Its reputation as a party island draws holidaymakers who are keen to enjoy Trawangan's spectacular ★ nightlife. As soon as the sunset cocktails are served

Farewell to the party island: backpackers waiting for the ferry

most of the cafés and bars turn the music up full volume; afterwards you can chill out to lounge music, dance to oldies or rave to techno beats. During the day, everything here revolves around the sea.
To keep misfortune far away from the Gilis, the *Mandi Sapa bathing ritual* is held on Trawangan every year at the end of the Islamic *Safar* month: hundreds of people carry offerings down to the sea and then they all go for a swim together. At the same time, newly hatched sea turtles are given their freedom. A local initiative has established a 😊 ● *turtle station (daily 8am–6pm | donations requested)* in front of Dino's Café in the northeast of the island with the aim of protecting these endangered animals. For romantics: you will have the best view of sunrise and sunset in front of the volcanoes on Bali and Lombok from the ● top of the small hill in the south of the island.

FOOD & DRINK

ART MARKET
(PASAR SENI) (138 C4) *(⌂ r4)*
In the evening, the locals and tourists taste their way through authentic Indonesian cooking at the numerous food stalls here. *Near the harbour | Budget*

ECCO BOUTIQUE CAFÉ
(138 C3–4) *(⌂ r3–4)*
Good coffee, fresh juices, homemade cake and bread, along with airy dresses and imaginative accessories. The purchases are packed in hand-folded paper bags. *Somewhat south of the harbour | tel. 0878 66 27 02 00 | Budget*

HORIZONTAL LOUNGE (138 C3) *(⌂ r3)*
Stylish restaurant-bar with lounger pillows on the beach. Western menu, barbecue and cocktails, lounge music. *North of the harbour | tel. 0370 6 13 92 48 | Moderate*

KARMA KAYAK (138 B2) *(⌂ q2)*
Enjoy tapas and sangria as you watch the sun go down. *At the north beach | tel. 0818 03 64 05 38 | Budget*

SCALLYWAGS ORGANIC SEAFOOD BAR & GRILL ☺ (138 C4) *(⌂ r4)*
Varied organic menu from breakfast to dinner; cosy setting. *In the southeast | tel. 037 06 14 53 01 | Moderate*

SHOPPING

In addition to your daily necessities, such as food, toiletries and postcards, it is also possible to buy local souvenirs and diving and snorkelling equipment here. More and more boutiques now also offer clothes and accessories. There is also an *art market (pasar seni)* held every evening at the harbour. Vendors sell cheap t-shirts, sarongs and handicrafts and there are local dishes on offer at the food stalls.

SPORTS & ACTIVITIES

There are many diving and snorkelling spots around the island where you can see turtles, manta rays and sometimes even small sharks. Some small firms also organise diving courses and tours on Trawangan but the larger ones are more reliable: *Dream Divers (tel. 0370 6 13*

During the day relaxing on the beach is called for

44 96 | www.dreamdivers-lombok.com | (138 C4) (𝄞 r4)), Blue Marlin Dive (tel. 0370 6 13 24 24 | www.bluemarlindive.com | (138 C4) (𝄞 r4)), Manta Dive (tel. 0370 64 36 49 | www.manta-dive.com | (138 C3) (𝄞 r3)).

The best angling spots for sports fishermen are in the northwest of the island. Scallywags (tel. 0370 6 14 53 01 | info@scallywagsresort.com | (138 C4) (𝄞 r4)) is one of the companies that organise trips. If you don't want to walk around the island on foot (around 3 hours), you can hire a horse (Stud Stables | tel. 0878 61 79 15 65 | (138 B5) (𝄞 q5)). There are yoga classes every day at Gili Yoga (tel. 0370 6 14 05 03 | www.giliyoga.com | (138 C4) (𝄞 r4)).

ENTERTAINMENT

The entire east coast of the island is full of places where you can go out and have fun. An official party plan lists those establishments where it is allowed to keep on rocking after 2am: Monday in the Blue Marlin (138 C4) (𝄞 r4), Wednesday in the Tir Na Nog (138 C5) (𝄞 r5) Irish Bar, Friday in Rudy's Pub (138 C4) (𝄞 r4) and Saturday in Sama-Sama (138 C3) (𝄞 r3). However, parties are now held almost every night at several locations – especially in the high season. Ask your hotel about the special events.

WHERE TO STAY

INSIDER TIP ▶ EXILE ☺
(138 A4) (𝄞 p4)
Ten simple bamboo bungalows with open-air baths in the quiet southwest that deliver a real island feeling; sunset bar with good music, ecological water and waste management. North of Sunset Point | tel. 0819 07 22 90 53 | lombokhomes@gmail.com | Budget

GILI ECO BUNGALOWS ☺
(138 B2) (𝄞 q2)
Seven comfortable two-room bungalows with open living rooms and private kitchens. Spacious garden, saltwater pool, restaurant and spa with organic products, coral project on the beach. In the northwest | tel. 0361 8 47 64 19 | www.giliecovillas.com | Moderate

Colourful turtle

LUCE D'ALMA RESORT ☺
(138 B3) (𝄞 q3)
Chic hotel – with pool, spa and Italian restaurant, its own hydraulic system and solar power – that offers its guests an ambience of modern luxury. 16 rooms | in the north, a little inland | tel. 0370 62 17 77 | lucedalmaresort.com | Expensive

PONDOK SANTI ☺
(138 A–B5) (𝄞 p–q5)
Twelve lovely bungalows in a well cared for, spacious grove of coconut palms on the south beach; education and environment project right behind the complex. Near Sunset Point | tel. 0370 6 14 51 86 | www.pondoksanti.com | Expensive

HOTEL VILA OMBAK (138 C5) (𝄞 r5)
Comfortable Sasak style complex. Pool, spa, restaurant, bar and dive school. New branch on the western beach. 60 rooms | in the southeast | tel. 0370 6 14 23 36 | www.hotelombak.com | Moderate–Expensive

TRIPS & TOURS

The tours are marked in green in the road atlas, the pull-out map and on the back cover

1 THROUGH BALI'S FERTILE HIGHLANDS

Starting from Ubud, travel around 60km (37mi) past temples and fruit orchards to the central highlands of Bali, where idyllic lakes and luxuriant nature await. After visiting the fairytale water temple Pura Ulun Danu Bratan, continue on past the Buyan and Tamblingan lakes, take a break for a dip at the Munduk Waterfall (remember your swimwear!), and the route goes via a serpentine mountain road down to the north coast. At the end of the day-long tour (a total distance of 93km/58mi) you can relax in some hot springs and meditate in Bali's only Buddhist monastery.

Set out from **Ubud → p. 66** early in the morning and travel via Singkerta and Blahkiuh to Sembung where you will reach the main road that leads northwards to Bedugul. You drive ever higher upwards past rice fields and fruit orchards until you arrive at **Candikuning** on **Bratan Lake → p. 50**, at an altitude of 1500m (4921ft). This region is considered the agricultural heart of Bali; the cool mountain climate makes it possible for fruit, vegetables and flowers to thrive here. Take some time and try the fresh mangoes and

Photo: Bratan Lake with the Pura Ulun Danu

Temples, traditional villages and tropical gardens: enjoy cultural highlights, pristine nature and spectacular views

strawberries or aromatic specialties such as spicy chicken with chillies, nutmeg, cloves, pepper and turmeric – all of these grow in the area – at the village market. The quaint **INSIDER TIP** **Eat, Drink, Love Coffee Shop** *(Budget)* in the middle of the market square is a good place to stop for a cup of delicious coffee. A little further down the road, the eleven-tier temple shrine of the **Pura Ulun Danu Bratan**

→ p. 50 can be seen on a small island in Bratan Lake its reflection gleaming in the water against the majestic setting of the mountains. It is no surprise that this is one of the most popular photo opportunities for tourists. The local people pray here to the goddess of the lake for water for their fields.

Now travel 5km (3mi) further to the north and then at Yehketipat turn off to the left and go to **Danau Buyan and Danau Tamblingan** → p. 50. The narrow road climbs high up above the northern shore of the glittering turquoise lake along coffee, clove and fruit orchards. The steep slopes of the **Gunung Batukaru** → p. 64 tower up on the opposite shore; in the north, the view sweeps down to the distant ocean.

A short distance after Tamblingan Lake, you arrive at the **Munduk Waterfall** (daily 8am–4pm | entrance fee 5000 Rp). A steep footpath (approx. 15 minutes) leads from the road through coffee and fruit orchards to a natural pool into which the waterfall plummets from a height of 15m (48ft). Here, you can have a refreshing swim before continuing on up the mountain. After a mile or so, you reach the restaurant of the ☀ **INSIDER TIP** **Puri Lumbung Cottages** (tel. 0362 70 12 88 71 | www.purilumbung.com | Moderate) in the village where you can stop for a lunchtime break. The fresh local dishes are accompanied by a breathtaking panoramic view. If you feel like enjoying the invigorating fresh mountain air a bit longer, you can spend the night in the award-winning ☺ Eco-Hotel (44 rooms | Moderate). Here, you will be able to learn a great deal about rice growing or go on a hike through the nearby mountain forest to the rustic lodge run by the hotel.

After Munduk, the narrow main road winds its way through small villages and plantations for around 20km (12mi). When you reach Bubunan, turn right towards **Banjar** → p. 49 and then right again at the village market. Shortly thereafter, a sign points the way to the left to the hot springs (Air Panas). Relax and enjoy a dip in the 38°C (80°F) warm water that flows out of carved spouts into the basin and is said to have healing powers.

Only ten minutes further away on the other side of the hill, you arrive at Bali's largest Buddhist temple and its only active Buddhist monastery the **Brahmavihara Arama** → p. 49, a popular meditation centre. Now, at the end of your tour, you can either meditate here or simply enjoy the peace and beautiful ocean views. After you leave the monastery, it is only 10km (6mi) to **Lovina** → p. 48, where there are many places to spend the night. If you decide to travel back to Ubud, you should take the road via Singaraja to Bedugul (approx. 2–3 hours).

2 A TEMPLE COMPLEX, THE RICE AREA AND UP BATUKARU

The 120km (75mi) long, one-day tour will take you from Bali's second largest temple complex in Mengwi to a stop in Tabanan, the most important rice cultivation area on the island. You then drive up the mighty Batukaru volcano to the mountain temple Pura Luhur Batukaru that is shrouded in myth. From there, you take a serpentine road to the

most beautiful rice terraces on the island. The breathtaking grand finale of the day is the sunset at Pura Tanah Lot.

After leaving Seminyak → p. 61, you travel 22km (14mi) to Mengwi → p. 65 and the Pura Taman Ayun that was founded in 1634. The expansive temple of the royal family of Mengwi is surrounded by a moat. Start your journey early in the morning so that you will be able to enjoy the beautiful garden in peace before the first tour groups arrive!

You now continue 7km (4mi) in the direction of Tabanan → p. 66, which is known as the rice granary of Bali. Shortly before reaching the little trading village, you will come across the small, but extremely interesting, ● Subak Museum (daily 8am–5pm | entrance fee 5000 Rp). The museum has a wealth of information about rice cultivation and the sophisticated irrigation system that follows democratic principles while remaining in tune with nature. The system was recognised by UNESCO and placed on its World Heritage List in 2012.

After leaving Tabanan, a road makes its way ever upwards for 23km (14mi) to the north to the verdant Batukaru → p. 64, the westernmost volcano on Bali and the islands second highest mountain. Hidden in a dense forest at an altitude of 825m (2707ft) lies the mystical mountain temple Pura Luhur Batukaru, one of Bali's six holiest places of worship. The shrines are dedicated to the mountain god and the spirits of the Bratan → p. 50, Buyan and Tamblingan lakes → p. 50.

Follow the main road around 2.5km (1.5mi) back to Wongayagede. A small winding road runs from here to the east passing first through banana, chilli and coffee plantations as far as ★ ⋇ Jatiluwih (access fee 10,000 Rp): here, with the clear view in the cool mountain air, you will have a fantastic panoramic view over dark-green rice fields to far in the south and down to the sea. The centuries-old fields nestle into each and every curve of the mountain slopes and present a perfect example of the Subak system you learnt about in the museum. Treat yourself to

Rice has been cultivated in the mountain region around Jatiluwih for centuries

a lunch break in the casual ☺ **Cafe Jatiluwih** *(tel. 0368 8152 45 | Budget)* and try the red rice that is cultivated here. It is served with fresh organic vegetables and fragrant **INSIDER TIP** red rice tea – produced by the Jatiluwih Organic Red Rice Farmers Association who continue to cultivate old rice varieties in a traditional manner without using any pesticides. The farmers believe that their natural way of growing the grain gives them a more direct connection to the rice goddess Dewi Sri. If you have enough time, you should go for a walk through the rice fields.

Next you drive via Gunungsari to Senganan, where you take a turnoff to the south to Tabanan another 25km (16mi) further on. If you still have enough energy, you can continue on for around another half an hour until you reach the **Pura Tanah Lot** → p. 65 sea temple, which is steeped in legend – despite the crowds, this is still one of the most beautiful places on Bali to enjoy the sunset.

3 SCENIC TOUR TO A SASAK VILLAGE IN NORTHERN LOMBOK

This day tour starts in Senggigi and leads about 85km (53mi) to the north of Lombok via the monkey forest at the Pusuk Pass and along beaches of black sand. After visiting a traditional Sasak village and Lombok's oldest mosque, you can unwind in the Rinjani Mountain Garden eco-resort and enjoy one of the most beautiful views the island has to offer. Then make a detour to the picturesque Sindanggila Waterfall before travelling back to the west coast to watch the sunset (total distance: 174km/108mi).

Leave **Senggigi** → p. 86 in the morning and drive via Ampenan towards the ☼ **Pusuk Pass**. You will reach **Gunung Sari** in time for the traditional morning market where you will be able to stock up on snacks for your trip or simply enjoy

Simple, but functional: it is pleasantly cool in the Sasak bamboo houses

the colourful hustle and bustle. You then head on to Sidemen. There are some palm sugar factories on the left side of the road: the farmers will be happy to show you how they produce palm sugar, palm wine *(tuak)* and liquor *(brem)* from the sweet sap of the Aren palm. When you reach the top of the pass, you will not only have wonderful views over forested mountain slopes as far as the sea and of the three Gili islands off shore, but will also be welcomed by a horde of hungry monkeys. Buy some bananas on the roadside before you get there to appease them and be sure to feed the leader first! You now continue on through pleasant villages and past black sand beaches until you reach a bumpy dirt road shortly before Sukadana that takes you to the traditional Sasak village of Segenter → p. 85. The people here still live the way they did hundreds of years ago in simple bamboo houses with clay floors. However, the building style and their language differ from those of the Sasak in the south of the island. If you make a donation at the entrance to the village, one of the residents will introduce you to everyday Sasak life, this usually also includes a brief visit to one of the houses.

Back on the main road, you drive on to Bayan → p. 84 and the oldest mosque on Lombok; it is a simple building constructed of wood and bamboo. It is said that one of the three holy men who brought Islam to Indonesia founded the first Islamic community on Lombok here in 1634. The people living in Bayan still see themselves as his direct descendants and are followers of the Wetu Telu faith with its blend of animistic, Hindu and Islamic elements. This is also true of the guardian of the sanctuary who can tell wonderful old stories – unfortunately, only in Indonesian (your driver can translate them for you). After the mosque, the main road makes

a sharp curve to the left and you continue straight ahead. A further 3.7km (2.3mi) up the mountain to a left curve and then turn sharp right to the entrance to the ☺ �☆ INSIDER TIP▶ Rinjani Mountain Garden *(tel. 0818 56 97 30 | Budget)*. The German owners have created a camping paradise with lush greenery, pools and all kinds of animal life here. For lunch, you can choose between Western snacks and spicy Sasak food and enjoy the view from the slopes of the Rinjani over the rice terraces down to the ocean. This is also an excellent starting point for wonderful trekking tours and the rice granary style bungalows will certainly tempt you to stay a bit longer. If you decide not to spend the night up here, you should leave and turn off towards Senaru → p. 83 shortly after Bayan. Most of the trekking tours to the Gunung Rinjani → p. 85 volcano start from this small mountain village. You should count on a tour taking an average of three days and can get more information in the office of the Rinjani National Park *(www.rinjaninationalpark. com),* which is also the headquarters of the mountain guide association. In contrast, the descent to the picturesque Sindanggila Waterfall → p. 86 that plummets down to the valley over two cascades only takes about twenty minutes. You will not need a guide for this, but if somebody offers his services and you accept, be sure not to pay more than displayed on the sign next to the entrance of the ☆ Pondok Senaru Restaurant *(daily | tel. 0370 62 28 68 | Budget)*. This is also a good place to have a cup of coffee with a view of the waterfall in the distance. Keep to the coastal road on your return trip. To make the sunset even more beautiful, you will have a spectacular view of the Gilis and – further off – of Bali's highest mountain, the Gunung Agung, from the bays south of Bangsal.

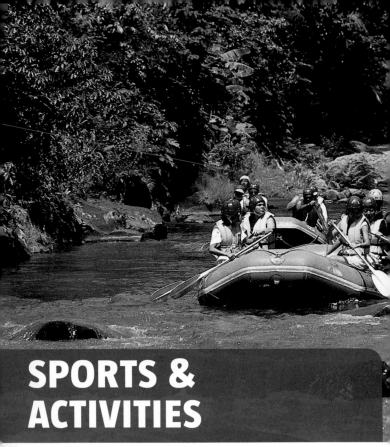

SPORTS & ACTIVITIES

Whether in Bali, Lombok or the Gilis: you will have an enormous range of leisure activities.

The focus is of course the sea with snorkelling, diving, sailing and surfing but there is also mountain biking, river rafting and – naturally – trekking tours on the volcanoes are very popular. Holidaymakers who are more interested in relaxation will find yoga classes, massages and spa treatments.

DIVING & SNORKELLING

Among the most popular dive and snorkel spots on Bali are Pulau Menjangan and Nusa Penida, as well as the shipwrecks covered with corals off the eastern coast. The Gilis are a real paradise for snorkellers and divers. The gentle currents make the reefs there just perfect for beginners. One of Lombok's best diving areas is Sekotong Bay in the southwest of the island. On Bali, courses are offered by *Water Worx Dive Center (Padang Bai | tel. 0363 4 12 20 | www.waterworxbali.com)* and *Eco Dive (Jemeluk | tel. 0363 2 34 82 | www.ecodive bali.com)*; on Lombok and the Gilis *Dream Divers (Senggigi/Gili Trawangan/Gili Air | tel. 0370 69 37 38 | www.dreamdivers.com)*; and – mainly in the south – **INSIDER TIP** *Divezone (Senggigi | tel. 0813 39 54 49 98 | www.divezone-lombok.com)*.

From the sea to the peaks: Bali, Lombok and the Gilis all offer a choice of activities and a variety of ways to relax

GOLF

The five golf courses on Bali and two on Lombok offer a superb selection. The *Bali Golf and Country Club* in Nusa Dua, the *Bali Handara Kosaido Country Club* in the mountains, as well as the *Bali Nirwana Golf Club* near Tanah Lot, are among the best golf courses in Asia. The comparatively new *Lombok Golf Kosaido Country Club* has a wonderful location with views of the Gilis. With the exception of the nine-hole *Balibeach Golf Course* in Sanur, all of the courses have eighteen holes. *Information and package deals under: www.99bali. com/golf and baliwww.com/golf*

HIKING & TREKKING

The main highlight for mountaineers is

the hike (least three days) up the *Gunung Rinjani* on Lombok. The *Gunung Agung* on Bali is also a real challenge for many. The half-day tour on the *Gunung Batur* is less demanding but just as impressive. On no account should you set out on one of these tours without a guide! The tour organisers include *Bali Sunrise Trekking (tel. 0818 55 26 69 | www.balisunrisetours.com)* and *Rinjani National Park (Senaru/Mataram | tel. 0370 6 60 88 74 | www.rinjaninationalpark.com).* The Swiss aid organisation ⏱ *Zukunft für Kinder (Future for Children) (tel. 0813 37 38 50 65 | www.zukunft-fuerkinder.ch/en)* organises trekking tours in the north of the Gunung Batur to provide support for village projects there.

HORSEBACK RIDING

Trotting through the villages and rice terraces in the hinterland, galloping along a beach or even going for a swim with the horses: there are many offers for horseback riding excursions on the beaches between Seminyak and Tanah Lot. *Island Horse Riding (tel. 0361 73 14 07 | www.baliislandhorse.com)* and *Bali Horse Adventure (tel. 0361 3 65 55 97 | www.balihorseadventure.com),* are well-known operators who organise children's camps as well as tours.

MOUNTAIN BIKING

Bike tours are very popular in spite of the tropical climate. The surroundings of Ubud are particularly suitable for cycling: the roads there are more or less intact and not terribly busy. You can easily cycle to the excursion destinations around Senggigi via the back roads in the surrounding area. The quiet roads on the southwest tip of Lombok are more adventurous but also very beautiful. Tours in small groups, starting in Ubud, are organised by *Bali Eco Cycling (tel. 0361 97 55 57 | baliecocycling. com)* and *Jegeg Bali Cycling Tours (tel. 0812 36 77 94 29 | www.jegegbalicycling.com).* INSIDER TIP *Mountain Bike Lombok (tel. 0819 99 09 71 26 | www.mountainbikelombok.com)* in Senggigi not only offers day trips but also interesting multiday tours.

The surf in the south of Lombok even challenges the experts

SPORTS & ACTIVITIES

RIVER RAFTING

The most popular is the roughly two-hour white water trip in an inflatable raft through the *gorges of the Ayung River* near Ubud. The tour on the *Telaga Waja River* on the Gunung Agung is more demanding – and you can be sure that your clothes will get wet! All of the organisers collect their guests from their hotels, such as *Bali Adventure Rafting (Ubud | tel. 0361 747 36 55 | www.bali-day-trip.com)* and *Sobek Bali Utama (Ubud/Kuta | tel. 061 28 70 59 | www.balisobek.com).*

SAILING

From a modern ocean-going catamaran to a traditional Bugis schooner: numerous operators offer a variety of sailing trips. Most cruises last from one day to a week and nearly all depart from Bali for the east. Nusa Lembongan is just one of the destinations of day trips; longer cruises also take in Lombok, Komodo and Flores *(such as with Condor Sailing | Hotel Uyah Amed | tel. 0363 23 46 62 | www.amed divecenter.com/sailing-bali* and *Sea Trek | Sanur | tel. 0361 27 06 04 | www.seatrek bali.com).* You can find more cruise offers under: *www.balicruises.com.* Some hotels, such as the Grand Hyatt in Sanur and the Four Seasons in Jimbaran, have Laser or Hobie cats available for hire for guests wanting smaller sailing adventures.

SPA TREATMENTS

Whether traditional Balinese massage, shiatsu or reflexology: at least one day of any holiday on Bali should be devoted to spa treatments. A massage on the beach lasting around one hour can be had for about 50,000 Rp – but it is worth spending more to be treated by trained masseurs in a spa and then being able to relax in a whirlpool bath. There are spas on every corner and in almost all the hotels on Bali; on Lombok, mainly in the larger establishments. You can find a selection of recommended spas at: *www.balispaguide.com.*

SURFING

The number of surfers on Bali and Lombok has increased in recent years: both islands are dream destinations for surfers. The surf rolls steadily on to the beaches from Kuta to Canggu – making them ideal for beginners. The huge waves at the southwest tip of Bali – for example at Padang-Padang, Bingin and Uluwatu – are best left to the experts!
The beaches in southern Lombok are still considered an insider tip; especially Mawi, Gerupuk and – for real experts – Desert Point on the southwest tip of the island. Surfing courses, board rentals and organised tours on Bali can be booked from the *Ripcurl School of Surf (Kuta | tel. 0361 73 58 58 | www.ripcurlschoolofsurf.com)* or *Padang Padang Surf Camp (Pecatu | Bukit Badung | tel. 0819 99 28 35 49 | www.bali surfingcamp.com),* and from *Kimen Surf (Jl. Raya Kuta-Mawun | Kuta | tel. 0370 65 50 64 | www.kuta-lombok.net)* on Lombok.

YOGA

Bali has developed into a centre of yoga over the past decade: yoga classes are included by many hotels (such as *Kumara Sakti* in Ubud | www.kumarasakti.com; *Samyoga* in Lovina | www.samyogabali. com). The *Bali Spirit Festival (www.bali spiritfestival.com)* is held in Ubud every year in March/April and attracts participants from all over the world. Lombok is not yet really riding the yoga wave; classes are limited to large hotels. There are also yoga classes on the Gilis: *(www.giliyoga. com; www.h2oyogaandmeditation.com).*

TRAVEL WITH KIDS

Bali in particular is a good holiday destination for children. The well-developed beaches and the exotic culture provide plenty of fun and entertainment: they can snorkel, explore the beach, experience exotic animals close up, and learn Balinese dances and arts and crafts. Families with older children will enjoy an active holiday on Lombok and the Gilis. As a precaution, you should make sure that you have medication for diarrhoea, fever and colds, as well as a disinfectant. In the tropics, even small wounds can quickly become infected and should be cleaned immediately. The strong sun means that children should always have sunblock on, wear a hat and drink a lot of liquids. You should also regularly apply mosquito repellent to avoid Dengue fever and malaria (particularly on Lombok and the Gilis) and sleep under a mosquito net. Arms, legs and feet should always be covered at dusk. The best places on Bali for spending a holiday with children are *Amed*, *Nusa Dua*, *Sanur* and *Ubud*. *Gili Air* is also very popular with families. Further information can found under: *www.baliforkids.com, www.baliparents.com* and *www.baliforfamilies.com*.

BUBBLEMAKER COURSES

Many providers organise snorkelling and diving courses for children. From the age of eight in a pool and in the open sea for those over ten. *Reef Seen Aquatics (tel. 0362 9 30 01 | www.reefseen.com)* offer a PADI Discover Scuba Diving course for those over ten while *Water Worx Dive Center (Padang Bai | tel. 0363 4 12 20| www.waterworxbali.com)* offer beginner courses for children over twelve.

INSIDER TIP DISCOVER THE RAINFOREST (131 D5) (*ØJ H4*)

The *Sarinbuana Eco Lodge* organises excursions for families to plantations and into the rainforest: everybody will learn a great deal about exotic animals and plants and also discover natural bathing spots and idyllic temples. Book in advanced via their website *Mount Batukaru | Tabanan | price from 200,000 Rp, free for children under the age of 15 | www.baliecolodge.com*

ELEPHANT SAFARI PARK
(135 D2) (*ØJ J5*)

In Bali's famous elephant park you can ride through the jungle on an elephant,

Climbing in the rainforest, riding elephants, exploring the underwater world – there are plenty of exciting experiences for children

watch them taking a bath and even see them painting. An exhibition provides a great deal of information and also exhibits the only mammoth skeleton in Southeast Asia. The profits are used to help preserve the Sumatra elephants that are threatened with extinction. You can stay overnight in the Park Lodge (25 rooms | tel. 0361 8 98 88 88 | www.elephantsafari parklodge.com | *Expensive*). Daily 8am–6pm | Jl. Elephant Safari Park Taro | Taro (20 minutes north of Ubud) | entrance fee US$65, children US$44, ride US$86, children US$58 (discounts for families) | www. baliadventuretours.com

TEMPLE DANCE AND HANDICRAFTS

Most children are fascinated by Balinese dances and temple festivals and would love to take part in them. Particularly in Ubud (135 D2) (*ω J–K5*), many introductory courses are offered where children can learn the basics of gamelan music and simple dance steps, as well as making batiks, carving or preparing temple offerings. The ARMA Museum (Jl. Raya Pengosekan | Ubud | tel. 0361 97 57 42 | www.armabali. com), Taman Harum Cottages (Jl. Raya Mas | Ubud | tel. 0361 97 55 67 | www.bali-hotel-taman-harum.com) and **INSIDER TIP** Mekar Bhuana Conservatory (Jl. Gandapura III/501x | Banjar Kesiman Kertalangu | Denpasar (135 D4) (*ω J6*) | tel. 0361 46 42 01 | www.balimusicanddance.com) are recommended for their courses.

WATERBOM PARK (134 C5) (*ω H7*)

Fun for all the family in an area covering over 9 acres. There are suitable entertainments for each age group, as well as a spacious pool complex and spa, and bars and cafés. Daily 9am–6pm | Jl. Kartika Plaza | Kuta | US$31, children to the age of 12 US$19 | www.waterbom-bali.com

FESTIVALS & EVENTS

No matter whether it is the Balinese New Year, the Islamic Feast of the Sacrifice or Christmas that is being celebrated, in Indonesia the major festivals of all the religions are public holidays.

NATIONAL HOLIDAYS

1 Jan Christian New Year; **Jan/Feb** *Imlek* (Chinese New Year); **March/April** *Nyepi* (Balinese New Year), Good Friday; **May/June** Ascension Day, *Waisak* (Buddhist New Year); **17 Aug** Independence Day; **25 Dec** Christmas

The *Muslim holidays* vary according to the Islamic lunar calendar (around 10 days shorter than ours). Ramadan ends with the *Idul Fitri (Lebaran)*, the most important Muslim festival in Indonesia (2015: 17./18.7, 2016: 6./7.7). Prayer sessions and torch-light processions are held on the night before the celebrations. All Indonesians have holidays and flights and hotels are often fully booked. Other holidays are: Islamic New Year, ▶ *Maulid Nabi* (Birthday of the Prophet), ▶ *Isra Mi'raj* (Night Journey and Ascension of the Prophet), ▶ *Idul Adha* (Islamic Feast of the Sacrifice).

BALINESE HOLIDAYS

Temple festivals on Bali are colourful events with processions, prayers, dancing and music. They are determined by the *Wuku* calendar that only has 210 days.

▶ ★ ● *Galungan/Kuningan* is the highlight of the Balinese year (2015: 15–25.7, 2016: 10–20.2. and 7–17.9). Ritual meals are prepared for the celebration that lasts ten days and there is dancing, music, shadow puppet theatre and processions. Drums, gongs and rattles drive out the evil spirits on the night before the New Year's festival ▶ *Nyepi*. The following day is one of fasting and meditation. Nobody is allowed to leave the house; traffic comes to a standstill – and there are also no flights!

▶ ● *Odalan* is the anniversary of a temple. During the day, the ancestors are revered with prayers and offerings, and there are performances in the evening. The many temples mean that there is always an Odalan festival taking place.

During the ▶ *Usaba Sambah Festival,* young men fight using Pandanus leaves as weapons in Tenganan while the young women swing in a wooden Ferris wheel.

Tradition meets the modern world: religious festivals, Balinese temple celebrations, processions, fertility rituals and cultural festivals

SASAK FESTIVALS

In addition to the Muslim holidays, the Sasak also celebrate festivals with animistic traditions. At full moon in February/March, they gather on the beaches in the south of Lombok to catch Nyale worms between the corals to celebrate ▶ *Bau Nyale*. This fertility ritual is something of a marriage market for young people.

The ▶ ● *Perang Topat* ('Rice Cake War') takes place at the beginning of the rainy season (usually in December) in the Pura Lingsar temple complex. Sasak and Hindus pelt each other with rice wrapped in palm leaves that are then buried to ensure a good harvest.

▶ *Perisean* fights are held in Mataram and Narmada in August. Two opponents battle each other with rattan sticks and bamboo shields; the first one to shed some blood, loses.

OTHER EVENTS

MARCH/APRIL

Yoga and meditation fans get together for the ▶ *Bali Spirit Festival* in Ubud.

JUNE/JULY

▶ *Bali Art Festival:* for one month, Bali's best artists show their skills in Denpasar. *www.baliartfestival.com*

AUGUST TO NOVEMBER

Speed, attitude and racing style are the main criteria in the ▶ *water buffalo races* in Jembrana in western Bali.

OCTOBER

▶ INSIDER TIP *Ubud Writers & Readers Festival:* authors have selected this as one of the most pleasant literature festivals. *www.ubudwritersfestival.com*

LINKS, BLOGS, APPS & MORE

LINKS

▶ www.bali.com Everything you need to know about your destination at a glance: accommodation links, community culture, ecotourism and offers ...

▶ beatmag.com/bali The hippest nightclubs, the trendiest organic menus and a lot of news about international celebrities on Bali can be found in the online biweekly entertainment guide

▶ www.jed.or.id The network for ecological village tourism offers holidays with local families in many traditional villages on Bali

▶ http://indonesia.travel/en/destination/73/bali History, sightseeing, spas, flora and fauna – the official tourism website has many tips to help you plan your Bali holiday

▶ giliecotrust.com The environmental protection organisation's beach cleaning, coral and sea turtle projects all need volunteers to support their efforts, see their website for details about how you can get involved

BLOGS

▶ janetdeneefe.com Restaurant owner Janet de Neefe not only founded the Ubud Writers & Readers Festival but also writes columns on Balinese cuisine that reveal a great deal about the cultural life of the island

▶ www.strangerinparadise.com The Australian journalist and garden architect Michael White takes on the role of a tactless tourist – and, in this way, gives entertaining insights into Balinese social life

▶ www.kutalombok.net The Indonesian photographer Fadil Basymeleh shows pictures of the landscape on Lombok and the Gilis

▶ www.thebalitimes.com Daily online English newspaper with local and international events, travel info and more

Regardless of whether you are still preparing your trip or already in Bali: these addresses will provide you with more information, videos and networks to make your holiday even more enjoyable

VIDEOS

▶ www.youtube.com/watch?v=SwLjk MCbgkk a slideshow entitled 'Best of Bali' as part of the GeoBeats travel series

▶ short.travel/bal2 Trailer to the documentary 'Cowboys in Paradise' by the Singaporean director Amit Virmani, who made himself unpopular with the Indonesian authorities with this depiction of male prostitution on Bali

▶ short.travel/bal3 The eight-minute film shows the fascinating underwater world of the Gilis

▶ short.travel/bal4 Performance by the dancer Ni Made Pujawati that gives an insight into classical Balinese dance and music

APPS

▶ Bali Map A free navigational app that has information about the main sights, cafés, hotels and other useful addresses

▶ Urbanesia Bali An app where travellers describe and evaluate their experiences on Bali with many anecdotes and photos. Free, suitable for Android devices

▶ Bali with Kids This is a helpful app for parents with tips about family-friendly hotels and activities for children

NETWORK

▶ www.tripbod.com A site where you can get to know the locals who take visitors by the hand and act as live travel guides – for a small fee, that is. Just enter 'Bali' in the 'marketplace' search function.

▶ friendsofgreenschool.org The 'friends' of the International Green School help newcomers with many tips on how to live (and survive) on Bali that will also be of interest to tourists

▶ www.travelforum.org/bali Online board where travellers exchange experiences and can ask specific questions about trips to Bali

TRAVEL TIPS

AIRPORT TAX

You have to pay an airport departure tax on leaving the island, the fee for international flights is 150,000 Rp and for domestic flights it is 30,000–40,000 Rp. According to the government, they plan to do away with additional fees in future.

ARRIVAL

The Ngurah Rai international airport near Denpasar is served by many international airlines, usually with a stopover in Singapore or Kuala Lumpur. There are also flights to Lombok from both cities: *Silk Air (www.silkair.com)* from Singapore, *Air Asia (www.airasia.com)* from Kuala Lumpur. The flight from Europe takes between 14 and 20 hours depending on the route and number of stopovers on the way.

RESPONSIBLE TRAVEL

It doesn't take a lot to be environmentally friendly whilst travelling. Don't just think about your carbon footprint whilst flying to and from your holiday destination but also about how you can protect nature and culture abroad. As a tourist it is especially important to respect nature, look out for local products, cycle instead of driving, save water and much more. If you would like to find out more about eco-tourism please visit: *www.ecotourism.org*

The flight from Denpasar to Lombok takes around 25 minutes: *Garuda Indonesia (www.garuda-indonesia.com), Lion Air (www.lionair.co.id)* and *Merpati (www.merpati.co.id)* have daily flights. Several airlines fly from Jakarta to Bali and Lombok – the cheapest is *Air Asia (www.airasia.com)*.

Ferries run constantly between all the Indonesian islands. For a list of the fares and crossings see *www.lombok-network.com/ferry_tarrif.htm*. There are also speedboats from Benoa or Padang Bai to the Gilis, with a stop in Teluk Nare in the northwest of Lombok *(various providers | gili-fastboat.com or gilifastboats. com)*. The speedboat operated by *Perama (www.peramatour.com)* provides a direct connection to Senggigi, Lombok's most important tourist destination.

There are several buses every day from Jakarta to Denpasar *(around 1200km/745mi | travel time 24 hours)* that make the crossing to Bali on the car ferry. The bus trip from Denpasar to Mataram takes about seven hours.

CAR HIRE

It is possible to rent mopeds and cars everywhere on Bali, as well as in Senggigi (Lombok); an international driving license is all that is necessary and the rates are very reasonable. Rental companies usually only offer their cars to drivers who are older than 21. A car with a driver who knows his way around (700,000 Rp/day) makes travelling much more pleasant. Take note: moped riders have to wear a helmet!

From arrival to weather

Holiday from start to finish: the most important addresses and information for your trip to Bali, Lombok and the Gili Islands

CONSULATES & EMBASSIES

USA CONSULAR AGENCY
Jl. Hayam Wuruk 310 | Denpasar 80235 | Bali | tel. 0361 23 36 05| Mon–Fri 8am–4.30pm

BRITISH HONORARY CONSULATE
Jl. Tirta Nadi 2 No. 20| Sanur | Bali | tel. 0361 27 06 01| Mon–Fri 8.30am–noon

CUSTOMS

Each person may bring 1 litre of spirits, 200 cigarettes or 100g of tobacco, into Indonesia. It is prohibited to bring drugs, firearms and pornographic material into the country. Electronic appliances must be taken out of Indonesia on departure. Export permission is required for antiques more than 50 years old and it is prohibited to export protected animals and plants (including corals!).

Travellers to the US who are residents of the country do not have to pay duty on articles purchased overseas up to the value of $800, but there are limits on the amount of alcoholic beverages and tobacco products. For the regulations for international travel for US residents please see *www.cbp.gov*

DRIVING

In Indonesia traffic drives on the left. Traffic on Bali and Lombok is chaotic and the roads are not especially good – particularly in the rainy season. The Gilis are car-free areas. If you decide to risk getting behind the wheel on your holiday, you should bear the following in mind: the person who has right of way, is the one who takes it. If somebody toots his horn, he wants to pass; if he flashes his lights, it means 'I come first'. Waving with the fingertips pointing down and the back of the hand to the front means 'come here'. Self-proclaimed 'parking attendants' usually help you in your efforts to get into or out of a parking space – for a few rupiahs.

BUDGETING

Coffee	£1/$1.60	for a cup
Nasi Goreng	£2/$3.30	for a serving
Petrol	£0.30/$0.50	for a litre
Car with driver	£37/$60	hire charge per day
Diving course	£45/$70	for an introductory course
Massage	£8/$13	for one hour

ELECTRICITY

The voltage is 220 Volt. Plug sockets are the two-pin variety; adapters are inexpensive and available everywhere.

EMERGENCY NUMBERS

Ambulance: *tel. 118*
Fire brigade: *tel. 113*
Police: *tel. 110*, police station in Kuta (Bali): *tel. 0361 75 15 98,* police station in Mataram (Lombok): *tel. 0370 62 23 73*

Horse carts *(cidomo)* are the cheapest means of transport on Lombok

Yani 9 | Selagalas | Mataram | tel. 0370 6 17 70 00 | harapankeluarga.co.id). If you fall seriously ill, it is best to fly out to Singapore. Medicines can be purchased in pharmacies *(apotik)* and drugstores *(toko obat)*.

IMMIGRATION

There are two kinds of visas for entry into Indonesia, certain passport holders must apply for a 'Visa in Advance' while others are eligible for the 'Visa on Arrival' option. In order to find out which is applicable you will need to contact your travel agent or an Indonesian embassy. Either way your passport must be valid for at least six months from date of arrival in the country. You fill out an arrival card on the plane and retain your departure card in your passport until you leave the country. A tourist visa can be extended once for 30 days.

HEALTH

It is recommend to be vaccinated against diphtheria, hepatitis A, polio, tetanus and typhoid. You should also have anti-malaria medication with you – especially if you are planning to visit Lombok and the Gilis. In addition, it is advisable to take out a health insurance that includes repatriation costs. Avoid drinking tap water and only eat ice cream and fruit in the better restaurants.

Many of the large hotels on Bali have a doctor in the house. The following clinics on Bali can be recommended for tourists: *BIMC Hospital Bali (Jl. Bypass Ngurah Rai No. 100X | Kuta | tel. 0361 76 12 63 | www. bimcbali.com)* and *International SOS Medical Clinic (Jl. Bypass Ngurah Rai 505X | Kuta | tel. 0361 71 05 05 | www.sos-bali. com)*. The best clinic on Lombok is the *Rumah Sakit Harapan Keluarga (Jl. Ahmad*

INFORMATION

Embassy of Indonesia USA – *2020 Massachusetts Ave NW | Washington DC 20036 | tel. 202 775 52 00 | www.embassy ofindonesia.org*
Embassy of Indonesia UK – *Visa and Consular Section | 38A Adams Row | London W1K | tel. 020 74 99 76 61| www. indonesianembassy.org.uk*

BALI TOURISM BOARD
Jl. Raya Puputan 41 | Renon | Denpasar | Bali 80235 | tel. 0361 23 56 00 | www. balitourismboard.org

INTERNET

Bali: *www.balispirit.com, blog.baliwww. com, hiddenbali.blogspot.com, visitubud. com, www.balivillas.com;* Lombok: *www. gotolombok.com, www.thelombokguide. com, www.lombok-network.com, visiting* lombok.blogspot.com; Gilis: *www.gili-blog. com, www.gili-paradise.com.*

INTERNET CAFÉS & WI-FI

Most of the hotels and restaurants on Bali, Lombok and the Gilis provide free Wi-Fi access; however, the connection is often poor in the more remote areas. There are internet cafés in all tourist resorts. USB modems for laptops can be bought from Smart or Telkomsel (from 400,000 Rp for 100 hours over 30 days) and other providers.

MONEY & CURRENCY EXCHANGE

The Indonesian currency is the rupiah (Rp). There are 50,100, 200, 500 and 1000 Rp coins, as well as 1000, 2000, 5000, 10,000, 20,000, 50,000 and 100,000 Rp notes. Many hotels calculate their prices in US$ or euros to compensate for the great fluctuation in the exchange rates. In such instances it is also possible to pay in these currencies and usually in rupiah at the current exchange rate but this can often result in a loss.

Banks are open from Mon–Thu from 8.30am–2pm, Fri 8.30am–11.30am. Moneychangers do business from 8am–8pm and often offer better rates than the banks (beware of cheats and always check the official rates!). There are cash dispensers (ATMs) in the larger towns where you can withdraw money using your EC or credit card and PIN code. The major hotels and shops also accept credit cards. Travellers' cheques, however, can usually only be cashed at a loss.

PERSONAL SAFETY

The most dangerous thing on Bali and Lombok is the traffic. You can feel safe wherever you go, even after dark. However, women travelling alone should be prepared for verbal flirting. Petty crime is mainly in the tourist resorts so it is a good idea to only have things you need with you including a copy of your passport and visa. Credit cards etc. are best kept in the hotel safe. Do not leave any valuables unattended on the beach or in your car!

CURRENCY CONVERTER

£	IDR	IDR	£
1	19,500	1,000	0.05
3	58,500	5,000	0.25
5	97,500	12,000	0.60
7	136,500	30,000	1.50
10	195,000	80,000	4
13	253,500	150,000	7.65
20	390,000	240,000	12.25
35	682,500	600,000	30.5
60	1,170,000	1,000,000	51

$	IDR	IDR	$
1	11,750	1,000	0.09
3	32,250	5,000	0.45
5	58,750	12,000	1.05
7	82,250	30,000	2.60
10	117,500	80,000	7
13	152,750	150,000	13
20	235,000	240,000	20.90
35	411,250	600,000	52.20
60	705,000	1,000,000	87

For current exchange rates see www.xe.com

PHONE & MOBILE PHONE

To call home from Bali dial 001 then your country code (UK 44; USA and Canada 1). Telephone calls are cheaper if you dial 007 before the country code when using the fixed-line network. If you do not have a telephone in your hotel, you can go to a *wartel* (telephone shop). The dialling code for Indonesia is 0062. Bali has the following area codes: (0)361 in the south, (0)362 in the north, (0)363 in the east, (0)365 in the west and (0)366 for Klungkung. Lombok and the Gilis can be reached under (0)370. You can make economical mobile telephone calls with an Indonesian prepaid card that can be recharged on every street corner.

PHOTOGRAPHY

As a rule, the local population has no objections to being photographed or filmed but you should still ask for permission beforehand. You should show particular restraint in temples and mosques; always ask for permission and never focus directly on the face of a priest. An extra fee is often charged for using a camera at special places of interest.

POST

Each major town has a post office *(kantor pos, Mon–Thu 8am–4pm, Fri 8am–11am, Sat 8am–12.30pm)*. It is also often possible to hand in your post at your hotel. Airmail *(pos udara)* takes one to two weeks to reach Europe. A postcard costs 7500 Rp, a standard letter 15,000 Rp.

PUBLIC TRANSPORT

Drivers offer their services on every street corner; the price is always subject to your negotiation skills. Hotels can also organise transport but they often charge for this service. Private shuttle buses, such as those operated by Perama Tours *(www. peramatour.com,* buy your tickets one day in advance from a travel agency), which have set timetables, are much less expensive. Residents prefer to take the small

local buses *(bemo, colt)* for a few cents – this is a real experience for anybody who is not afraid of close contact and inquisitive questions. Unfortunately, the tourist transport business has almost done away with most of the minibuses in the south of Bali. You can order a taxi *(Blue Bird Bali: tel. 0361 70 16 21, Blue Bird Lombok: tel. 0370 62 70 00)* in the major centres. On Lombok and the Gilis, the *cidomos* and *dokars* (one-horse carriages) are great for travelling short distances. There are fixed prices for *cidomos* on the Gilis and they are only subject to negotiation in exceptional cases.

TIME

Bali, Lombok and the Gilis are in the Central Indonesian time zone (WITA), which is eight hours ahead of Greenwich Mean Time (GMT) (seven hours during daylight saving time).

TIPPING

Ten per cent is appropriate in a restaurant if a service charge is not included – in that case, just leave some small change. A chauffeur will be pleased to receive 50,000 Rp after a day trip and – depending on how satisfied you were – you can give a guide at one of the main sights 10,000–20,000 Rp.

WHAT TO WEAR

Skimpy clothing is not appropriate on any of the islands. This also applies to men – especially on official occasions such as appointments with the authorities. Knees and shoulders must always be covered when visiting temples; you can rent a sarong at the entrance for a donation or fixed fee if you do not have a suitable wrap-around with you. Light cotton clothing with long sleeves and legs is also the best protection against sunburn and mosquito bites. And, although some female tourists sun themselves topless in Kuta: bathing in the nude is forbidden in Indonesia.

WHEN TO GO

The best period is the dry season from May to October. It rarely rains continuously in the rainy season from November to April but the heavy tropical downpours often result in flooding in the interior of the country and may limit your activities. The temperature is around 30°C (86°F) throughout the year but it can be considerably cooler in the mountainous regions.

WHERE TO STAY

From homestays to luxury hotels – there are all kinds of accommodation options on Bali. Homestays and *losmen* (guesthouses) frequently have no air conditioning and only an Indonesian *mandi* or ladle bath. In the small venues it is often possible to negotiate a discount for longer stays.

Many of the large hotels and villa complexes provide first class service but charge in US dollars. It is cheaper if you make your internet booking well in advance. Holiday homes with inclusive prices are becoming increasingly popular with families and groups.

WEATHER IN DENPASAR

	Jan	Feb	March	April	May	June	July	Aug	Sept	Oct	Nov	Dec
Daytime temperatures in °C/°F												
	30/86	30/86	30/86	31/88	31/88	30/86	30/86	31/88	31/88	32/90	32/90	30/86
Nighttime temperatures in °C/°F												
	22/72	23/73	23/73	23/73	23/73	23/73	22/72	22/72	22/72	23/73	23/73	23/73
Sunshine hours/day												
	8	10	10	10	9	9	9	10	11	10	10	10
Precipitation days/month												
	12	10	7	4	3	3	3	3	2	3	5	10
Water temperatures in °C/°F												
	28/82	28/82	28/82	29/84	28/82	28/82	27/81	27/81	27/81	27/81	28/82	29/84

USEFUL PHRASES INDONESIAN

PRONUNCIATION

To facilitate pronunciation: in general, the penultimate syllable is stressed.
The vowels are spoken the same length. Diphthongs **ai**, **au**, **oi** are pronounced
as two separate vowels when they appear inside a word, but as one sound
when at the end of a word.

c	like the **ch** in **ch**eers
e	in syllables that are not at the end: unstressed **e** as in st**e**rn
	in syllables at the end of a word: stressed **e** as in r**e**d
	final syllables: short **a** as in for**ay**
ng	eng like the soft **ng** in si**ng**ing
ngg	eng like the hard **ng** in bi**ng**o
ny	nye like the **ny** in ca**ny**on (similar to the ñ sound in Spanish)
kh	kha lie the **ch** in lo**ch**
sy	sya like the **sh** in **sh**oe or **sh**ip

IN BRIEF

Yes/No/Maybe	ya/tidak/mungkin
Thank you/Please	Terima kasih!/Tolong! *(asking for help)*
	Silakan! *(offer/invitation)*
	Sama-sama! *(don't mention it)*
Excuse me, please	Maaf!
May I ...?/Pardon?	Boleh ...?/Bagaimana?
I would like to .../have you got ...?	Saya mau .../Apa ada ...?
How much is ...?	Berapa harga ...?
I (don't) like this	Saya (tidak) suka.
good/bad/broken/doesn't work	baik/jelek/rusak/tidak jalan
too much/much/little	terlalu banyak/banyak/sedikit
Help!/Attention!/Caution!	Tolong!/Awas!/Hati-hati!
ambulance/police/fire brigade	ambulans/polisi/pemadam kebakaran
Prohibition/forbidden	larangan/dilarang
danger/dangerous	bahaya/berbahaya
Can I take a picture of you/here?	Apa saya boleh memotret Anda/di sini?

GREETINGS, FAREWELL

Good morning!/	Selamat pagi *(until 11am)*/
afternoon!	siang *(11am–3pm)*

Kamu berbicara bahasa Indonesia?

"Do you speak Indonesian?" This guide will help you to say the basic words and phrases in Indonesian.

Good evening!/night!	sore *(3–6pm)*/malam *(from 6pm)*!
Hello!/Goodbye!/See you!	Halo!/Sampai jumpa!/Dada!
My name is ...	Nama saya ...
What's your name?	Siapa nama Anda?/Siapa nama kamu?
I'm from ...	Saya dari ...

DATE & TIME

Monday/Tuesday	Senen/Selasa
Wednesday/Thursday	Rabu/Kamis
Friday/Saturday	Jumat/Sabtu
Sunday/working day/holiday	Minggu/hari kerja/hari raya
today/tomorrow/yesterday	hari ini/besok/kemarin
hour/minute	jam/menit
day/night/week	hari/malam/minggu
month/year	bulan/tahun
What time is it?	Jam berapa?
It's three o'clock	Jam tiga.
It's half past three.	Jam setengah empat.
quarter to four	Jam empat kurang seperempat
quarter past four	Jam empat lewat seperempat

TRAVEL

open/closed	buka/tutup
departure/arrival	keberangkatan/kedatangan
toilets/ladies/gentlemen	kamar kecil/wanita/pria
(no) drinking water	(bukan) air minum
Where is ...?/Where are ...?	Di mana ...?
left/right/straight ahead/back	kiri/kanan/terus/kembali
close/far	dekat/jauh
bus/minibus/taxi	bis/bemo/taxi
(bus) stop/cab stand	haltebis/pangkalan taxi
street map/map	peta
train station/harbour	stasiun/pelabuhan
airport	bandara/airport
I would like to rent ...	Saya mau ... sewa.
a car/a bicycle	mobil/sepeda
a boat	kapal
petrol/gas station	pompa bensin
petrol (gas)/diesel	bensin/solar
breakdown/repair shop	kendaraan rusak/bengkel

FOOD & DRINK

Could you please book a table for tonight for four?	Tolong reservasi satu meja untuk empat orang nanti malam.
The menu, please.	Minta menu.
Could I please have ...?	Apa saya tolong bisa mendapat ...?
bottle/glass	botol/gelas
knife/fork/spoon	pisau/garpu/sendok
with/without ice/sparkling	pakai/tanpa es/gas
vegetarian/allergy	vegetaris/alergi
May I have the bill, please?	Saya mau bayar.
bill/receipt/tip	bon/kwitansi/tip, uang rokok

SHOPPING

Where can I find...?	Di mana ada ...?
I'd like .../I'm looking for ...	Saya mau .../Saya cari ...
Do you put photos onto CD?	Apa Anda bisa membakar foto di CD?
pharmacy/chemist	apotik/toko obat
bakery/market	toko roti/pasar
shopping centre/department store	pusat pembalanjaan/mall
food shop	toko bahan makanan
supermarket	supermarket
photographic items/newspaper shop	toko foto/kios koran
kiosk	warung/kios
100 grammes/1 kilo	seratus gram/satu kilo
expensive/cheap/price	mahal/murah/harga
more/less	lebih banyak/lebih sedikit
organically grown	organik

ACCOMMODATION

I have booked a room.	Saya sudah reservasi kamar.
Do you have any ... left?	Apa masih ada ...?
single room	kamar untuk satu orang
double room	kamar untuk dua orang
breakfast/half board	sarapan/makan pagi dan malam
full board	tiga kali makan
at the front/seafront	menghadap kedepan/menghadap laut
lakefront	menghadap danau
shower/sit-down bath/balcony/terrace	shower/mandi/balkon/teras

BANKS, MONEY & CREDIT CARDS

bank/ATM/pin code	bank/ATM/pin
I'd like to change ...	Saya mau menukar ...

cash/credit card	tunai/kartu kredit
change	uang kembalian

HEALTH

doctor/dentist/paediatrician	dokter/dokter gigi/dokter anak-anak
hospital/emergency clinic	rumah sakit/bantuan medis darurat
fever/pain	demam/rasa sakit
diarrhoea/nausea/sunburn	menceret/mual/terbakar matahari
inflamed/injured	inflamasi/luka
plaster/bandage	plaster/perban
ointment/cream	salep/krim
pain reliever/tablet/suppository	obat anti-nyeri/tablet/uvula/pil taruh

POST, TELECOMMUNICATIONS & MEDIA

stamp/letter/postcard	perangko/surat/kartu pos
I'm looking for a prepaid card for my mobile.	Saya cari kartu prabayar untuk HP.
Do I need a special area code?	Apa saya perlu kode khusus?
socket/adapter/charger	stopkontak/adaptor/charger
computer/battery/rechargeable battery	komputer/baterai/aki
at sign (@)	at
internet address (URL)/e-mail address	alamat internet/alamat email
internet connection/wi-fi	akses internet/WiFi
e-mail/file/print	email/file/cetak

LEISURE, SPORTS & BEACH

beach	pantai
sunshade/lounger	payung/kursi malas
low tide/high tide/current	air surut/air pasang/arus

NUMBERS

0	nol/kosong		11	sebelas
1	satu		12	dua belas
2	dua		80	delapan puluh
3	tiga		90	sembilan puluh
4	empat		100	seratus
5	lima		200	dua ratus
6	enam		1000	seribu
7	tujuh		2000	dua ribu
8	delapan		10000	sepuluh ribu
9	sembilan		½	setengah
10	sepuluh		¼	seperempat

NOTES

FOR YOUR NEXT HOLIDAY ...

MARCO POLO TRAVEL GUIDES

- PACKED WITH INSIDER TIPS
- BEST WALKS AND TOURS
- FULL-COLOUR PULL-OUT MAP
  AND STREET ATLAS

ROAD ATLAS

The green line ___ indicates the Trips & Tours (p. 98–103)
The blue line ___ indicates The perfect route (p. 30–31)

All tours are also marked on the pull-out map

Photo: Gunung Agung

Exploring Bali, Lombok and Gili Islands

The map on the back cover shows how the area has been sub-divided

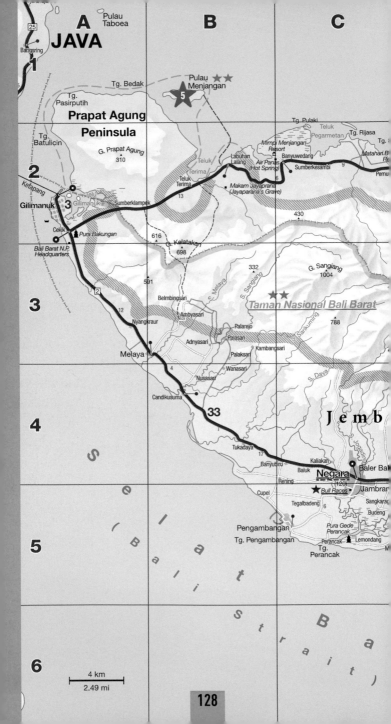

JAVA

Pulau Taboea

25

Bangsring

A

1

Tg. Bedak

Pulau Menjangan ★★

5

Tg. Pasiruputih

Prapat Agung Peninsula

Tg. Batulicin

G. Prapat Agung
310

Tg. Pulaki

Teluk Pegarmetan

Tg. Rijasa

Tg.

Mimpi Menjangan Resort

Banyuwedang

Matahari B Re

Ketapang

Teluk Terima

Labuhan Lalang

Air Panas (Hot Spring)

Sumberkesambi

9

Pemu

2

Gilimanuk

Teluk Gilimanuk

3

Teluk Terima

13

6

Sumberklampek

Makam Jayaprana (Jayaparana's Grave)

Cekik

Pura Bakungan

Bali Barat N.P. Headquarters

616

Kelatakan

698

430

591

332

G. Sangiang
1004

Belimbingsari

Taman Nasional Bali Barat ★★

3

12

Nyangkraur

Ambyasari

Palarejo

Palasari

788

2

Adnyasari

Palaksari

Kambangsari

Wanasari

Melaya

4

Nusasari

33

Candikusuma

2

4

Tukadaya

17

Kaliakah

J e m b

Banyubiru

Baluk

Negara

Baler Ba

120

Rening

Cupel

★ **Bull Races**

Jambran

Tegalbadeng

6

Sangkarag

Budeng

Pengambangan

Pura Gede Perancak

Tg. Pengambangan

Perancak

Lemondang

5

Tg. Perancak

M

S e l a t   B a l i   (B a l i   S t r a i t)

6

4 km
2.49 mi

D   **E**   **F**

1

LAUT BALI
(Bali Sea)

2

Pulaki

▲ Pura Pulaki ★

▲ Melanting

Tg. Gondol

Gondol

10

64

11

Gerokgak

Celukanbawang

Brombong

Kalisada

Tegal
lenga

Ba

6

3

B u l e l e n g

489

G. Musi
1224

1031

G. Mesehe
1344

998

1057

1182

1412
P. Patas

982

1156

701

582

(Bali Barat National Park)

481

4

507

662

742

812

621

a

Pesantran

Sembung

Penyaringan

Mendaya
lagintukad

Tegalcangkring

Douhmarga

Mendaya

Yehbuah

Yehembang

kuning

Airsatang

Pura
Rambut Siwi

10

Yehsumbul

Asahduren

5

5

Pesinggahan

Pulukan

Pekutatan

Pantai Medewi
(Medewi Beach)

2

53

10

Guml

6

i

A B C

1
4 km
2.49 mi

LAUT BALI
(Bali Sea)

★ SINGA

2

Pantai Lovina
(Lovina Beach)
Lovina
Tuk
Antura
Wanupanggang 4
Kalibukbuk
Temukus
21
Damai
Lovina
Pengastulan
Pegayaman
Labuhan Haji
Genit
Umaanyar
Seririt
Dencarik
Brombong
Kalisada
10
Tangguwesia
Banjar Tega
Singsing
Air Terjun
(Sinsing Falls)
Tegal-
lenga
Banjarasem
Patemon
Bubunan
Johanyar
Banjar
Brahmavihara Arama
Kaldpaksa
260
Ringdikit
Kornala Tirtaa
(Hot Springs
Air Panas)
623

Buleleng

489
730
982
Rangdu
Mayong
Bestala
Busungbiu
Keberan
Pedewa
Tunjuk
12
Kayuputih
Banyuatis
Kedis
Pelapuan
922
S. Mendaun
Gobleg
Air
Mur
572
Munduk
(700)
R.
Fi
Umajero

3

742
812
852
Pucaksari
800
Pertigaan
Kemosing
798
Bantiran
43
Pupuan
Blahmantung
Air Terjun
Blahmantung
10
Blahmakuan

4

621
Tista
Munduk
Mengenu
733
617
7
12
Sahi
Pujungan
Padangan
Galiukir
Kebonpadangan
734
Batungsel
Pempatan
Sanda
19
Sarinbuana
Mengenu
Anyar
5
Asahduren

5

502
Badingkayu
Penginadan
445
Blimbingtegal
Blimbing
Kebonjaju

Ta

53
2
10
Gumbrih
Pangeragoan
Pancoran
Nagasari
Angkah
Ampadan
Tinggading
Antegana
8
Pegemelan
Lumbung
282
4
Manseke
Berembeng
154
Selemadeg
Jeljin
194
M

6

Kutuh
Suraberata
Balian
Beach Resort
Lalanglingah
Antosari
Balera
Serampingan
Mambang
Dukuhpulu
10
Seka
Cekik
Wi

134

130

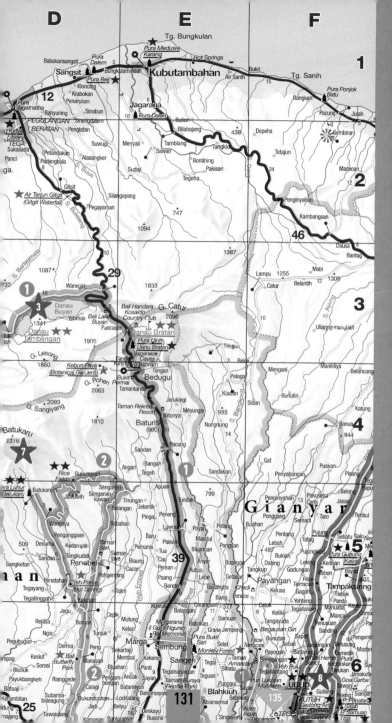

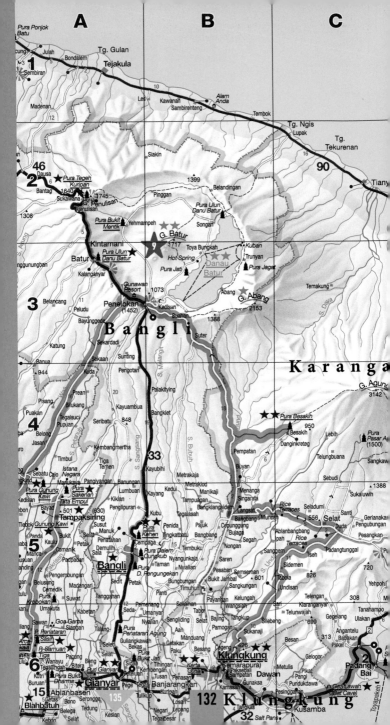

A **B** **C**

Pura Ponjok
Batu

1
Julah
Bondalem
Tejakula
Tg. Gulan
Sembiran
Madenan
Les
Kawanan
Sambirenteng
Alam
Anda
Tembok
Tg. Ngis
Lupak
Tg.
Tekurenan
90
Tiany

2
46
Dausa
Bantag
Pura Tegeh
Kuripan
1640
Sukawana
Penulisan
PENULISAN
1745
1308
Yehmampeh
Pinggan
1399
Belandingan
Pura Ulun
Danu Batur
Songan
Pura Bukit
Mentik
Kintamani
G. Batur
3717
Toya Bungkah
Kuban
Batur
Pura Ulun
Danu Batur
Hot Spring
Danau
Batur
Trunyan
Pura Jagat
Kalanganyar
Gunawan
Resort
1073
Pura Jati
Abang
Temakung
S. Daya

3
Belancang
11
Peludu
Penelokan
(1452)
Kedisan
Buahan
G. Abang
2153
Bayunggede
Suter
1388
B a n g l i
K a r a n g a
Katung
Sekardadi
Banua
944
Sekaan
Sunting
Pengotan
G. Agung
3142

4
Prean
Bilukang
Kuda
Kayuambua
Palakitiyng
Bangkiet
Pura Besakih
Besakih
950
Lebih
Pura
Pasar A
(1500)
Puakan
Tegalsuci
Pupuan
Seribatu
848
Danginkreteg
Pisang
Timbul
Istana
Negara
Kembangmertha
Tiga
Temen
Kayubihi
Metrakaja
Pempatan
Buyan
6
Telungbuana
Sebudi
1388
Sangkaw

33
Sebatu
Pura Gunung
Kawi
Pura
Sakenan
Tirta Empul
Tampaksiring
Gunung Kawi
501
630
Lumbuan
Kikian
Penglipuran
Kayang
Kedui
Manikaji
Tampuagan
Bangkiangsidem
Menanga
Singarata
Rice
Terraces
Seladumi
Sukaluwih
556
Santi
Gerianaka
Pengubungan

5
Bayad
Bukit
Selat
Petak
Susut
Manuk
Demulih
Sala
Pura
Kehen
Cempaga
Penida
Tingkattbatu
Tegalasah
Pajuk
Bangbang
Cepunggung
Bujaga
Bangbang
Muncan
Langsat
Segah
Nongan
Iseh
Sanggem
Sidemen
Padangtunggal
Duda
Selat
Pesangkan
720

Manca
Comanik
Padpadan
Bangli
Pura
Dalem
Gungkub
Nyangunkaja
Nyalian
Saren
Pesaban
Semerman
601
Sangkungan
Tabola
826
Undisan
Pengembungan
Belusung
Cemedik
Suwat
Pura
D. Pengungekan
Petak
Bungbungan
Timunun
Bukit Jambal
Payangan
Kelungah
Sari
Telengan
308
Yehpoh

Umakuta
Madangan
Tanggahan
Sedit
Panti
Wangsian
Tangkup
Sibleng
699
Telunwajah

6
Krobokan
Umalanta
Kabetan
Seda
Umanyar
Pemenang
Selisihan
Nyalian
Tabri
Bajing
Pamogan
Sukanaji
Cegeng
Metulis
Gelogor
Antangelu
Babakan
Pakel
313

Goa Garba
Sawan
P. Penataran
Sasih
Siangan
Talang
Selat
Guliangkawah
Bekas
Sengliding
Aan
Getakan
Manduang
Paku
Besang
Klungkung
Semarapura
Paksebali
Kamasan
Dawan
Besan
Pikat
Pangi
Pundukdawa
Karangasem
Padang
Bai

Arca
kaid
Pura
Peniataran
Tiga
P. Samuan
Tiga
Pacung
Beng
Bitera
Pura
Bukit Jati
Thingan
Tusan
Penasan
Kerta Gosa
Gelgor

15
Kutri
Buruan
Pura Bukit
Dharma
Tegallinggah
Gianyar
Sidan
Pege
Tegal
Banjarangkan
Kamasan
Sampetan
Guksa
Pesinggahan
Goa Lawah
(Bat Cave)
Ulakan

Blahbatuh
Getas
Belega
Ablanbasen
Bono
Serongga
Tedung
Belega
Kesian
135
Tulikup
Negari
Lepang
Tegalbesar
Kesian
132 K l u n g k u n g
Kusamba
Salt Pans
Padang
Bai

A   B   C

1

734
Blimbing-tegal
130
Kebonjajung
Sarinbuana Eco Lodge
Wongaya
Penganggaam
Babahan
Pinga
Luwus
Baru
Poya

T a b a n a n
509
Denuma
Sandan
Sangketan
Kedampal
Tengkudak
Penebel
Taman Sari
Suman-taye
Pemasis
Biaung
Cacan
Paian
Tua
Perean
39
Kutup

Ampadan
Tinggading
Penatahan
Yeh Panas (Hot Spring)
Pohgending
Tajen
Pang
Bepteh
Balangan

Nagasari
Angkah
282
Lumbung
Antegana
Manseke
Selemadeg
194
Timpag
Kesiut
Sorosi
Derma
Peng
Sekartaji
Kekeran
Kelaci
Ol
Tunjuk
Marga
Margarana
(I Gusti Ngurah Rai Memorial)
Sembung
Sangeh

2
Berembeng
Antosari
154
Jelidh
Gadungan
Blubuk
Butterfly Park
Wanasari
Membal
Panti
Kekeran
Tegalnarungan
Reptile Park
Taman Buraya
(Reptile Park)

10
Bajera
Serampingan
Megati
Payukbangkeh
Rianggede
Calagi
Pengam-bengan
Ancak
Batannyuh
Sayan
Badung
Banjarsayan
Baha

Cekik
Betjah
Mambang
Dukuhpulu
Wangkal
Bantas Meliling
Keramibitan
Batuaji
Mandung
Subamia-baleaguung
Dukunduahan
Jadi
Loddalang
Belyu
167
Denkayu
Busana
Penan

Antap
Seka
Santanbuah
Tista
Lumajang
Samsam
25
Tabanan
(150)
Pangkung-pearhu
Kamasan
Banjaranyar
Baira
Pura Taman Ayun
Munggu
Mengwi
Dajanpe
Cemen

Tg. Bulungdaya
Klecung
Banjarbongan
Tangguntiti
Jaketabel
Krambitan
Puri Anyar
Pangkungarung
Serongsuk
Tariahbang
Subak Museum
Pupuan
Bringkit
Kapal
Nambaikoja

Beraban
Bumbang
Puri Agung
Stronggo
Demung
108
Karipan
Kediri
Pasekan
Pura Sada
Muncan
Perangkelod

Tegaltemu
Penarukan
Tanahpegat
Bantas-bandung
Pandakmerangg
Kumpayah
Pura Puseh
(75)
Lukluh
Sempidi
Negara

3
Klating
Klatingdukuh
Kalanganyar
Wansera
Pamesan
Simpangan
Sangiang
Kabakaba
Tangeb
16
Taman

Sudimara
Yehgangga
Bengkelkawan
Mundeh
Belalang
Panti
Douhjero
Buwit
Balangpuseh
Gaji
Dalung
Umicandi
Gede
Padang-bali
Tegallalang
Umahany

Beraban
Nyanit
3
Krobokan Munggu
Sedahan
Danginsema
Kabakaba
Tibueneng
Celuk
Krobokan
Uluma

Tanah Lot
Pura Tanah Lot
Bali Nirwana Resort
2
Dukuh
Sangiangan
Kangkang
Kayutulang
Jambe
LEMINTANG
BALUN

Mengening
Pengembungan
Pererenan
Canggu
Villa Puri Dewata
Kerobokan
Buana
PADANGSAMBIAN
PAMEDILAN

4
Seseh
Banjartengah
Pelambungan
Anyar Kelod
Pengubengan
JEMATANG
BUWAGAN

Berawa
Umalas
Padang sambu
ABIANTIMBUL

Batubelig
Petitenget
Taman
Basangkasa
13
PEDLING
Dukuh

Pura Petitenget
Padang
6
Seminyak
Kepawon
Glogor
Jangut
Amb

Legian
Plasa
Suwitngg

SAMUDERA
Teluk Kuta
Kaleng
5

Kuta
Waterbom Park
Tuban
Kebonganan

INDONESIA
Abiyankuta
Tg. Be

5
(Indian Ocean)
Ngurah Rai Int. Airport
Pengederan
Labuha
Beno

Teluk Jimbaran
Jimbaran
Four-Seasons
Mumbul

Balangan Beach
Dreamland Beach
Pura Belangan
Cengiling
Simpangan
10

Bingin Beach
Universitas Udayana (UNUD)
Kampi

Padang Padang Beach
Suluban Beach
Labuansait
Bukit Badung
Baking
Bangbang
Bargol
Kampi

6
Suluban
Pura Luhur Uluwatu
1
Uluwatu
Pecatu
202
Kutuh
130
Sawa

4 km
2.49 mi
Nyang Nyang Beach
Pura Mas-Suka
Bali Cliff Resort
Pura Batu Pageh
Ungasan

Bali

Lombok

A **B** **C**

1

10 km
6.21 mi

2

Gili Trawangan
Nusa Gili
Gili Meno
Gili Air
Gili Trawangan
Pantai Medana
Offshore Spring
Sira
Pantai Sira
Bangsal
Menggala
Teluk Nara
Teluk Pandanan
Tanjung Serunggal
Pantai Nipah
Nipah
Malimbu
Tanjung Rumbak
Bentek
Baun Pusuk
(Pusuk Pass)
Kliu
Mangsit
Karangdangan
Senggigi
Pura Batu Bolong
Teluk Senggigi
Batu Bolong
Batu Layar
Kekait
Gunung Sari
Pura Segara
Selaparang Airport
Rembiga
Ampenan
MATARAM
Cakranegara
Sweta
Mapakbelatung
Nyamarai
Gunung Pengsong
Banyumulek
Gapuk
Rumak
Kediri
Ubung
Bilekere
Kayangan
Sidutan
Upak
Mayung
Luk
Tanjung Papak
Papak
Gondang
Rempek
Penjor
Karang Kates
Jambianom
Bentek
Anjah
Pemenang
Terangan
Medain
Medana
Pura Medana
Tanjung
Kali Sega
Batulilir
Koppang
Baturunggu
Monkey Forest
Gn. Argapu
Gn. Dudu
Gn. Pusuk
Gn. Menining
Kebonbaru
Gn. Menuting
Gn. Pongkar
Air Nyet
Pura Lingsar
Pura Suranadi
Sesao
Suranadi
Narmada
Taman Narmada
Pura Kalasa
Pringgarat
Perina
Aikn
Sukarara
Jelantik
Bundu
Puyung
Leneng
Ungga
Darek
Batujar
Penujak

3

4

Padang Bai (Bali)
Labuhan Benoa (Bali)
Muara Besar
Tanjung Bebra
Desert Point
Selegong
Bangko Bangko
Gili Anyaran
Gili Asahan
Gili Gede
Pengawisan
Gili Nanggu
Labuhan Poh
Temeran
Sekotong Barat
Ketapang
Taun
Cemare
Labuhan Lembar
Endok
Bakongdasan
Gerung
Riocung
Ranggagata
Plambik
Pancor
Sepolong
Sekotong Timur
Gn. Mereje
Kabol
Bonder
Mangkung
Kateng
 Pangan
Selong Belanak
Raml
Ketapang
Teluk Labuan kuweng
Pelangan
Gn. Embit
Ramoutpetung
Mecanggah
Batugendeng
Sekotong Tengah
Kelep
Sayong
Jago
Tendaun
Tojang
Keling
Semenanjung Sekotong
Slodong
Gn. Panggang
Blongas
Sepi
Suare
Timbal
Montong sapah
Selong Belanak
Gn. Barbojot
Mawi
Mawun
Tamba
Are Goling
Kur
Tanjung Batubukun
Tanjung Marmadi
Tanjung Mekaki
Tanjung Batujonggat
Teluk Panggang
Pengantap
Tanjung Ujunglangit
Teluk Trawas
Tanjung Glopoh
Teluk Tampa
Tanjung Pengulu

5

6

I N D I A N O

Padang Bai (Bali)
Labuhan Benoa (Bali)

Selat Lombok

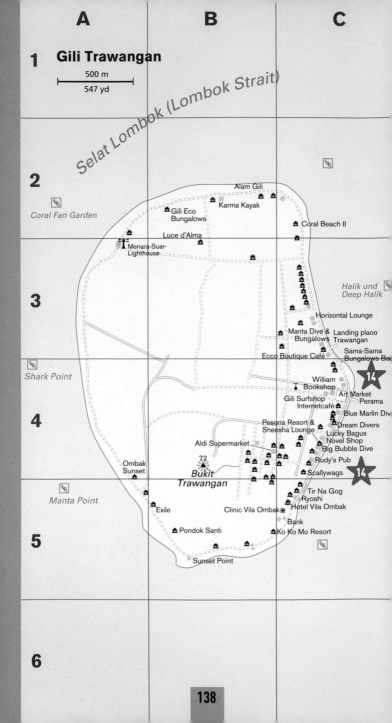

Gili Trawangan

500 m
547 yd

Selat Lombok (Lombok Strait)

Coral Fan Garden

Alam Gili

Karma Kayak

Gili Eco Bungalows

Coral Beach II

Luce d'Alma

Menara-Suar-Lighthouse

Halik und Deep Halik

Horizontal Lounge

Manta Dive & Bungalows

Landing place Trawangan

Sama-Sama Bungalows Bar

Ecco Boutique Café

Shark Point

William Bookshop

Art Market

14

Perama

Gili Surfshop
Internetcafé

Blue Marlin Dive

Dream Divers

Pesona Resort & Sheesha Lounge

Lucky Bagus Novel Shop
Big Bubble Dive

Aldi Supermarket

Rudy's Pub

72

Scallywags

14

Ombak Sunset

Bukit Trawangan

Tir Na Gog
Ryoshi

Manta Point

Hotel Vila Ombak

Exile

Clinic Vila Ombak

Bank

Pondok Santi

Ko Ko Mo Resort

Sunset Point

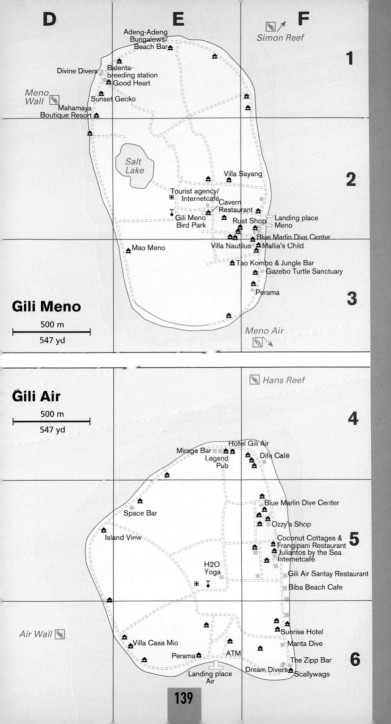

D **E** **F**

Adeng-Adeng
Bungalows/
Beach Bar

Simon Reef

1

Divine Divers

Balenta-
breeding station
Good Heart

Meno
Wall

Sunset Gecko

Mahamaya
Boutique Resort

Salt
Lake

Villa Sayang

2

Tourist agency/
Internetcafé

Cavern
Restaurant

Gili Meno
Bird Park

Rust Shop

Landing place
Meno

Blue Marlin Dive Center

Mao Meno

Villa Nautilus

Mallia's Child

Tao Kombo & Jungle Bar

Gazebo Turtle Sanctuary

Gili Meno

Perama

3

500 m

547 yd

Meno Air

Hans Reef

Gili Air

4

500 m

547 yd

Hotel Gili Air

Mirage Bar

Legend
Pub

Difa Café

Blue Marlin Dive Center

Space Bar

Ozzy's Shop

Island View

Coconut Cottages &
Frangipani Restaurant
Juliantos by the Sea
Internetcafé

5

H2O
Yoga

Gili Air Santay Restaurant

Biba Beach Cafe

Air Wall

Sunrise Hotel

Villa Casa Mio

Manta Dive

Perama

ATM

The Zipp Bar

Dream Divers

Scallywags

6

Landing place
Air

KEY TO ROAD ATLAS

Dual carriage-way
Straße mit zwei
getrennten Fahrbahnen

Thoroughfare
Durchgangsstraße

Important main road
Wichtige Hauptstraße

Main road
Hauptstraße

Other road
Sonstige Straße

Carriage way, track
Fahrweg, Piste

Mule-track, footpath
Karrenweg, Fußweg

Roads under construction
Straßen in Bau

♀ 49 ♀ Long distances in km
Großkilometer

↑ 10 ↑ Short distances in km
Kleinkilometer

Main line railway
Fernverkehrsbahn

Car ferry
Autofähre

Shipping route
Schifffahrtslinie

Swamp
Sumpf

Mangrove
Mangrove

Coral reef
Korallenriff

Route with
beautiful scenery
Landschaftlich besonders
schöne Strecke

◄ 15% ► Important gradients
Bedeutende Steigungen

DENPASAR Administrative capital
Verwaltungssitz

✈ Airport
Verkehrsflughafen

⊕ Airfield
Flugplatz

★★ **UBUD** Culture
Kultur
Worth a journey
Eine Reise wert

★ **Krambitan** Worth a detour
Lohnt einen Umweg

Landscape
Landschaft

★★ *Danau Bratan* Worth a journey
Eine Reise wert

★ *Kebun Paya* Worth a detour
Lohnt einen Umweg

☀ ⩗ Important panoramic view
Besonders schöner Ausblick

National park, nature park
Nationalpark, Naturpark

4807 ▲ Mountain summit with height
in metres
Bergspitze mit Höhenangabe
in Metern

(630) Elevation
Ortshöhe

▲ Monastery, temple,
shrine (Buddhist)
Kloster, Tempel,
Heiligtum (buddhistisch)

▲ Temple, shrine
Tempel, Heiligtum (hinduistisch)

⌘ Palace, castle
Schloss, Burg

⚑ Monument
Denkmal

/ Waterfall
Wasserfall

∩ Cave
Höhle

⁝ Ruins
Ruinenstätte

▪ Other object
Sonstiges Objekt

ⵎ Golf-course
Golfplatz

△ Youth hostel
Jugendherberge

🖻 ⛱ Bathing beach
Badestrand

🤿 Diving
Tauchen

Trips & Tours
Ausflüge & Touren

Perfect route
Perfekte Route

★ **1** **MARCO POLO Highlight**
MARCO POLO Highlight

INDEX

This index lists all places, sights and destinations featured in this guide. Numbers in bold indicate a main entry.

CREDITS

WRITE TO US

e-mail: info@marcopologuides.co.uk

Did you have a great holiday?
Is there something on your mind?
Whatever it is, let us know!
Whether you want to praise, alert us to errors or give us a personal tip – MARCO POLO would be pleased to hear from you.
We do everything we can to provide the very latest information for your trip.

Nevertheless, despite all of our authors' thorough research, errors can creep in. MARCO POLO does not accept any liability for this. Please contact us by e-mail or post.

MARCO POLO Travel Publishing Ltd
Pinewood, Chineham Business Park
Crockford Lane, Chineham
Basingstoke, Hampshire RG24 8AL
United Kingdom

PICTURE CREDITS

Cover photograph: Rice fields near Petulu (Laif: Hub)
Anantara Hotels, Resorts & Spas (17 top); BALI Stand UP Paddle (16 bottom); Oka Dipurra (16 centre); DuMont Bildarchiv: Raupach, Schwarzbach (42); R. Dusik (20, 43, 76, 116); Huber: Picture Finders (18/19); © iStockphoto.com: webphotographeer (16 top); laif: hemis.fr (2 centre top, 7, 82, 85), Hub (1 top); Laif/hemis fr: Seux (106); H. Mielke (53); mauritius images: Alamy (front flap left, front flap right, 2 centre bottom, 2 bottom, 3 top, 4, 10/11, 32/33, 49, 56, 60, 63, 74/75, 78, 81, 86, 90/91, 92, 95, 96, 97, 100/101, 102, 112 top, 112 bottom, 126/127, 141), ih (J. W. Alker) (9), Kugler (111), Vidler (88); C. Schieber (15); C. Schott (1 bottom); sks: S. Scappin (17 bottom); O. Stadler (2 top, 3 centre, 5, 6, 8, 12/13, 22, 24/25, 26 right, 27, 28, 28/29, 30 left, 30 right, 34, 37, 41, 59, 65, 68, 70, 73, 98/99, 110/111); T. Stankiewicz (55); M. Thomas (45, 46, 50, 67, 72, 108/109, 109, 110, 113); White Star: Reichelt (3 bottom, 29, 39, 104/105, 108)

1st Edition 2015
Worldwide Distribution: Marco Polo Travel Publishing Ltd, Pinewood, Chineham Business Park, Crockford Lane, Basingstoke, Hampshire RG24 8AL, United Kingdom. E-mail: sales@marcopolouk.com
© MAIRDUMONT GmbH & Co. KG, Ostfildern
Chief editor: Marion Zorn
Author: Christina Schott, editor: Ulrike Frühwald
Programme supervision: Ann-Katrin Kutzner, Nikolai Michaelis
Picture editor: Gabriele Forst
What's hot: wunder media, München
Cartography road atlas & pull-out map: © MAIRDUMONT, Ostfildern
Design: milchhof : atelier, Berlin; Front cover, pull-out map cover, page 1: factor product münchen
Translated from German by Robert Scott McInnes; editor of the English edition: Margaret Howie, fullproof.co.za
Prepress: M. Feuerstein, Wigel
Phrase book in cooperation with Ernst Klett Sprachen GmbH, Stuttgart, Editorial by Pons Wörterbücher

DOS & DON'TS

A few things to bear in mind while on holiday in Bali

DO AVOID CHEAP ALCOHOL

Be wary of very cheap cocktails and spirits: they are often mixed with home-brewed palm or rice liquor that is manufactured unprofessionally or adulterated with poisonous additives. In recent years there have been cases of methanol poison – something that can even lead to death.

DON'T BUY ANY DRUGS

Hashish, ecstasy and magic mushrooms are offered for sale on every street corner in the tourist centres. On no account should you enter into any such deals! There are severe penalties for drug possession and in particularly serious cases conviction can even lead to a death sentence. No exceptions are made for foreigners.

DON'T PUT YOUR FEET UP

Feet are considered impure and should not be put up in public. You should not climb around on walls or statues in temples for the same reason.

DO BE SENSITIVE ABOUT CORAL REEFS

Avoid walking on coral reefs, doing so not only damages the highly sensitive ecosystem but also is also dangerous. Corals can be very sharp and there are also poisonous coral creatures that should not be touched.

DO TREAT SACRED SPRINGS WITH RESPECT

Anybody who desecrates a sacred spring by bathing in it will not only attract the wrath of the gods but also have to cover the costs of the spiritual purification that is necessary afterwards.

DON'T EAT TURTLES

Although officially only allowed on special occasions, some dealers offer turtle eggs, meat and shell for sale. These animals are under threat of extinction so you should definitely decline any offers! The same applies to shark fins, which are cut off of the animals while they are still alive.

DON'T DISTURB TEMPLE CEREMONIES

Tourists are welcome to attend most ceremonies as long as they know how to behave themselves properly: wear a sarong with a sash, don't walk around in front of those praying, never sit higher than the priest and never point a camera directly in somebody's face.

DO BE PATIENT

If you become impatient waiting or bargaining you will achieve nothing at all! As a rule, you will get much further with a friendly smile. If at all possible, you should turn down any forms of bribery.